VATICAN MUSEUMS
ROME

Newsweek/GREAT MUSEUMS OF THE WORLD

NEW YORK, N.Y.

**GREAT MUSEUMS
OF THE WORLD**

Editorial Director—Carlo Ludovico Ragghianti
Assistant—Giuliana Nannicini
Translation and Editing—Editors of ARTNEWS

VATICAN MUSEUMS
ROME

Texts by:

Gigetta Dalli Regoli

Decio Gioseffi

Gian Lorenzo Mellini

Roberto Salvini

Design:

Fiorenzo Giorgi

Published by

NEWSWEEK, INC.
& ARNOLDO MONDADORI EDITORE

1st Printing 1969
2nd Printing 1971
3rd Printing 1972
4th Printing 1973
5th Printing 1974
6th Printing 1978
7th Printing 1979
ISBN: Clothbound Edition 0-88225-239-9
ISBN: Deluxe Edition 0-88225-214-3

Library of Congress Catalog Card No. 68-20026

PREFACE

DEOCLÉCIO REDIG DE CAMPOS
Inspector of the Vatican Museums

The ensemble of the Pontifical Monuments, Museums and Galleries is undoubtedly one of the most important in the world, because of the quality of the works and because the settings in which they are preserved and which were created for them (Sistine Chapel, Raphael's Stanze, the Borgia Apartment, etc.) are architectural works of equal historic and artistic importance.

The Vatican Museums had their origin in the private collections of Cardinal Giuliano della Rovere, which he brought to the Apostolic Palace and exhibited in the Belvedere Garden of Innocent VIII (1482–1492), when he was elected Pope in 1503 and took the name of Julius II (1503–1513). This typical humanistic open-air museum, which was then enriched by the munificence of Leo X (1513–1521), Clement VII (1523–1534) and Paul III (1534–1550), included such famous statues of antiquity as the *Apollo,* appropriately called *Belvedere,* the *Torso,* the marble group of the *Laocoön*, the *Tiber* and the *Nile.* The Middle Ages passed on to us the spiritual, literary, political and juridical heritage of the Western classical world, before the coming of Christ. The Church recognized the eternal human value of this precious written heritage, to which the popes of the Renaissance added that of the figurative arts, creating the museums alongside the libraries, and the first of these in Europe was opened by Sixtus IV (1471–1484), on the Capitoline hill in Rome.

The museum of Julius II (or Garden of the Statues, as it was called) was liberally open to scholars and artists, but one could not properly say to the public. Indeed a sign by the entrance warned the "profane" to keep away. It was only in the 18th century, under the influence of Winckelmann in archeology and of Lanzi in the history of art, that Benedict XIV (1740–1758) carried out the project of Clement XI (1700–1721), and founded the Museo Sacro of the Vatican Library, where objects of medieval minor art of inestimable historic and artistic value are preserved. For brevity we shall mention only the *Reliquary of the True Cross* (10th century), from the Sancta Sanctorum of the Lateran; the *Rambona Diptych* (9th century); a silk fragment with the *Annunciation* (7th century); an icon of the 11th century showing St. John Chrysostom; and reliquaries in Limoges enamel from the 13th to the 16th centuries. Benedict XIV's successor, Clement XIII (1758–1769) added the Museo Profano to the Museo Sacro; the former is dedicated to the minor arts of antiquity, but it also contains precious relics of classical Roman painting, such as the fresco fragments illustrating episodes from Homer's Odyssey and the so-called Aldobrandini Wedding picture (a nuptial scene), both of the Augustan period, i.e., 1st century A.D. In recent times, to these two museums of the Vatican Library has been added the Salone Sistino, constructed originally by Sixtus V (1585–1590) as the new reading room of the library, and now devoted to the exhibition of some of its most famous treasures: the so-called *Joshua Roll,* an example of Byzantine miniature painting done between the 7th and

9

8th centuries; the two Virgil codices called the *Vatican Virgil* and the *Roman Virgil,* of the 4th and 5th centuries respectively; and other precious manuscripts.

The ensemble of the Vatican Museums became truly magnificent with the creation of the Museo Pio-Clementino in the splendid halls arranged by the architects M. Simonetti and G. Camporesi under Popes Clement XIV (1769–1774) and Pius VI (1775–1799), to house such famous works as the *Venus of Cnidus,* copy of a celebrated statue by Praxiteles, 4th century B.C.; the *Sleeping Ariadne,* copy of a Hellenistic original of the 2nd or 3rd century B.C.; the *Apollo Belvedere,* copy of an original Greek bronze of the 4th century B.C. (one of the first ancient statues brought to the Vatican by Julius II); the original of the *Laocoön,* recently restored by F. Magi, who re-attached the right arm of the old man, and who has dated the work as of the 2nd century B.C.; finally, *Bathing Venus,* copy of a statue by Doidalse, a Greek sculptor who lived between the 3rd and 2nd centuries B.C.

An important section was added to the museums by Gregory XVI (1831–1846) with the Museo Gregoriano-Etrusco, which includes the *Acroterion* of the 5th century B.C.; the Orientalizing large fibula of the 7th century B.C.; and the stupendous amphora by Exekias, masterpiece of one of the best Athenian vase painters of the 6th century B.C., illustrating *Achilles and Ajax Playing Dice.*

The Pinacoteca is one of the most recent sections of the Vatican Museums, having been founded by Pius VI after the return from Paris, under the Treaty of Tolentino, of the works of art removed by the French. The most ancient and unusual painting is in the first room; it represents a *Last Judgment* and is signed by the Roman painters, Johannes and Nicolaus, who lived between the end of the 11th and the beginning of the 12th centuries. Giovanni di Paolo, Sienese artist of the 15th century, is the author of an *Annunciation* painted on a panel and used to bind an account book of the municipality of Siena; the inscription records the names of the "wise men," and there are also their coats of arms and the date 1444–1445. The Pinacoteca includes a polyptych by Giotto, formerly in St. Peter's; *Madonna and Child* by Vitale da Bologna; a dramatic *Crucifixion* by Niccolò Alunno, follower of Carlo Crivelli (15th century); *Madonna and Child Enthroned with St. Dominick and St. Catherine* by Fra Giovanni da Fiesole, called Fra Angelico; *Angel Musician,* a large fresco fragment from the destroyed 15th-century apse of the Basilica of the SS. Apostoli, in Rome, a work by Melozzo da Forlì; a fresco by the same artist representing the *Inauguration of the Vatican Library,* which was detached from the wall of one of the original rooms of the library and mounted on canvas; and *Madonna Enthroned with Saints* by Pietro Perugino. In the large hall devoted entirely to Raphael may be seen his *Coronation of the Virgin,* the *Madonna of Foligno,* the *Transfiguration* — which he left unfinished — and the splendid series of tapestries with scenes from the *Acts of the Apostles,* woven in Brussels from his cartoons as decorations for the Sistine Chapel. The *St. Jerome* of Leonardo da Vinci is one of the rare jewels of the Vatican; another gem of the Pinacoteca is Caravaggio's *Deposition of Christ,* often considered his most significant work.

SISTINE CHAPEL — Built between 1475 and 1483 by Giovannino de' Dolci after the plan of Baccio Pontelli for Sixtus IV, the Sistine is the "official" private chapel of the Pope, in which besides the various religious functions, the conclaves for the papal elections are held. The singers' gallery of the famous Sistine Choir and the graceful carved marble balustrade are the works of Mino da Fiesole, Giovanni Dalmata and Andrea Bregno (15th century). The pavement is a handsome example of 15th-century Roman mosaic work, of the type called *opus Alexandrinum*. The 12 frescoes, disposed in two cycles of six on the main walls, represent scenes from the *Life of Moses,* liberator of Israel (on the left), and scenes from the *Life of Christ,* liberator of all mankind (on the right), in accordance with an ancient iconographic tradition by which Moses prophetically prefigures the Messiah. The two series begin on the altar wall, but the first two frescoes — the *Finding of Moses* and the *Nativity,* both by Perugino — were destroyed in the 16th century to make room for Michelangelo's *Last Judgment.* Restoration at present being carried out has revealed on the bands of the marbled frames the Latin *tituli* of the various frescoes, of which until now there was no documentary evidence whatsoever. The vault of the Sistine Chapel was painted by Michelangelo between 1508 and 1512, by order of Julius II, a nephew of Sixtus IV, who had by intuition seen in the great sculptor, who had never painted in fresco, the only artist capable of undertaking the colossal enterprise of decorating the immense ceiling (until then provisionally painted blue). After discarding his first project, which comprised the twelve Apostles seated on thrones between the lunettes (where the Prophets and Sybils are now to be seen), Michelangelo decided to connect his work with the compositions existing on the walls, where the historical era of mankind — before (Moses) and after (Christ) the Redemption — is represented, by painting on the ceiling the proto-history, so to speak, of the humankind. His subject was the Genesis of the world, according to the Bible, from the beginning of the Creation to the Flood and the resumption of life on the earth devastated by the Flood, with the family of Noah.

The *Last Judgment,* on the altar wall, was executed under Paul III, from 1535 to 1541. Above, Christ as Judge appears in the guise of a Christianized god of classical antiquity (Apollo-Hercules), with his right hand raised in the gesture of condemnation. Close to him are the Madonna, St. John the Baptist, with the goatskin around his waist, and St. Andrew with his distinctive cross (seen from behind). On the other side are St. Peter, with two enormous keys, symbolizing his mission as the Vicar of Christ; next to him is St. Paul, and at Christ's feet, St. Lawrence and St. Bartholomew. The latter holds his own skin in his hand (this martyr was flayed), and the flaccid face of the skin is a caricature portrait of Michelangelo himself. To the left of this central group are the women; to the right the men, among whom may be distinguished Simon of Cyrene carrying Christ's cross, St. Sebastian, St. Catherine and other martyr saints. Below, in the middle zone, are seen the risen dead ascending to Heaven; in the center, a cave full of devils; to the right, the entrance to Hell, with Charon's boat, represented as described by Dante, and Minos, the infernal judge, to whom the painter has given (also adding long ass's ears) the appearance of Paul III's Master of Ceremonies, Monsignor Biagio Martinelli of Cesena, who had ventured to criticize his work! The *Last Judgment* of the Sistine Chapel is the *Dies Irae* of the dying Renaissance, and the most impressive statement of the Catholic Reformation, a movement desired by Paul III and later achieved in the Council of Trent.

Toward the end of 1508 Julius II entrusted to Raphael, then 25 years old, the decoration of the so-called Stanze, which had been built by Nicholas V in the 15th century and were intended by him to serve as the pontifical apartment. Various 15th-century painters (among them Piero della Francesca) had worked there, but their compositions were destroyed to make room for new frescoes, except for part of the ceiling decorations.

Raphael began painting in the Stanza della Segnatura (1508–1511), originally planned as the Pope's private library, as shown by the themes of the frescoes which represent in historical form (side walls), allegorical form (rectangles of the vault) and symbolic form (medallions), the three fundamental Platonic Ideas: the True (theological in the so-called *Disputation of the Sacrament,* and philosophical in the *School of Athens*), the Good (in its subjective source, the Virtues, and in its objective expression, the Law, symbolized in the frescoes by the *Pandects* and the *Decretals*) and the Beautiful (in *Parnassus*) — all conceived in accordance with the concepts of Christian Platonism then in great favor, especially through the work of Marsilio Ficino. Julius II had a direct hand in the choice of subjects.

The so-called *Disputation of the Sacrament,* on the west wall, shows the glory of the Church Triumphant, adoring the Holy Trinity in Paradise. Saints and Prophets flank the central group of Christ with the Madonna and St. John the Baptist. Above is God the Father making the gesture of benediction, and between heaven and earth is the dove of the Holy Ghost with angels bearing the four Gospels. In spiritual communion with the Church Triumphant above is the Church Militant on earth, represented by the assembly of saints, popes and theologians adoring the Divinity on earth in the daily miracle of the consecrated Host displayed on the altar. Numerous portraits distinguish these figures, including those of Dante and Savonarola to the right and that of Fra Angelico in the far left corner. The *School of Athens,* on the opposite wall, shows an ideal meeting of the most famous philosophers of ancient Greece, presided over by Plato and Aristotle — the two Princes of the classical thought of the West — under the vaults of a majestic basilica, designed by Bramante, fellow-countryman of Raphael, who at the time was building the new Vatican basilica, whose appearance is anticipated here, as in an architectural dream. Here too are many portraits. Plato is Leonardo da Vinci. Euclid is Bramante (drawing with a compass on the ground), and next to him in the far right corner are Raphael himself (with a black cap on his long hair) and Sodoma, the painter who assisted him in his first work at the Vatican (wearing a white cloak). Seated alone in the middle of the scene is Heraclitus, an ideal portrait of Michelangelo, imitated from the Prophet Isaiah in the Sistine Chapel. Around the neck of the figure of Euclid-Bramante appears the signature R.V.S.M., or *Raphael Urbinas Sua Mano,* meaning "Raphael of Urbino, by his hand." Three cardinal virtues — *Fortitude, Prudence* and *Temperance* (in the lunette to the right of the preceding fresco) — symbolize the moral content of the Law represented by the two scenes to the sides of the window below, executed in part by Raphael's assistants. To the left is *Tribonian Delivering the Pandects to Justinian;* to the right, *Gregory IX Receiving the Decretals from the Jurist St. Raymond of Pennafort* (the Pope is a portrait of Julius II). The supreme cardinal virtue, *Justice,* is represented above the others in the ceiling medallion.

12 *Parnassus* (in the lunette of the facing wall) shows Apollo absorbed in playing a lyre

(the *lira da braccio* type) on top of the sacred hill; around him are the nine Muses, while in a slow movement from left to right, passes the solemn procession of the great poets of antiquity (Homer, Ennius, Virgil, Sappho), the Middle Ages (Dante and Petrarch) and the Renaissance (Boccaccio, Ariosto, Castiglione, Sannazaro and Tebaldeo).

On the ceiling, above the *Disputation,* are the rectangular composition of *Adam and Eve* and the medallion with the symbolic figure of *Theology;* above the *School of Athens, First Motion* and *Philosophy;* above the *Virtues,* the *Judgment of Solomon* and *Justice;* above *Parnassus,* the scene of *Apollo and Marsyas* (executed by another hand) and *Poetry.* In the next Stanza is the representation of the *Expulsion of Heliodorus from the Temple of Jerusalem* (1512–1514) which illustrates an episode in the Old Testament: Heliodorus, who has come to steal the treasure held for widows and orphans in the Temple of Jerusalem, is chased out by angels, one of the most beautiful of whom is on horseback. To the left appears Julius II in procession, as if he were passing in front of the fresco and had paused to look at it with pleasure. The scene alludes to the efforts of the Pope to free the State of the Church from usurpers.

The *Miraculous Mass of Bolsena* portrays the miracle that took place in 1263 at Bolsena when a doubting priest while saying Mass saw the consecrated Host bleed, a prodigy in memory of which the feast of Corpus Domini was instituted. Julius II — a portrait worthy of Titian in its chromatic splendor — is shown in adoration, to the right of the altar.

The *Deliverance of St. Peter* (from prison in Jerusalem) is a triumph of light that anticipates the luminous magic of Rembrandt by more than a century and a half. The scene intends to signify the divine protection accorded to the Church in the person of its Head, the Vicar of Christ. The same protection, accorded to the Holy City of Rome, episcopal seat of St. Peter's successors, is symbolized in the fresco of *The Meeting of Attila and St. Leo.* The left-hand half of this painting is predominantly the work of Raphael, and only in part by his students. The historical meeting between the King of the Huns and the Pope took place near Mantua, but the artist, with poetic license, has set it before the gates of Rome, the barbarian's goal, which is saved by the apparition of St. Peter and St. Paul who dissuade him from continuing on his course of devastation. The Pope here is a portrait of Leo X, Julius II having died (1513) when Raphael had barely begun to paint the wall, which is why Leo, that is Giovanni de' Medici, is portrayed twice, once as cardinal, on a mule, and again as pope on the *Chinea,* the white horse that the Neapolitan kings offered to the pope as their feudal lord.

Raphael's Logge make up the façade of the old Vatican Palace looking toward Rome. They were begun by Bramante for Julius II and completed by Raphael, who directed their decoration, which was carried out with a free hand by his students (1514–1518). The ornamentation (stucco work and painted grotesques) was inspired by the Roman wall decorations of Nero's Golden House, which had been recently rediscovered. The ceiling compositions represent scenes from the Old Testament, and for this reason the cycle is sometimes called Raphael's Bible.

Of the frescoes executed between 1492 and 1495 by Pinturicchio and assistants in 13 the Borgia Apartment for Alexander VI, the most beautiful is reproduced here: the *Disputation of St. Catherine of Alexandria* (before the Emperor Maximinus, prior to her martyrdom). Pinturicchio was a fellow student with Raphael at Perugino's school, but never went much beyond the level of a pleasing decorator, and in this quality he is triumphant here.

The Chapel of Nicholas V, private chapel of the popes, is also well known as the Chapel of Fra Angelico, the devout Dominican painter who — from 1447 to 1450 — covered the walls with admirable frescoes of scenes from the lives of the two saintly deacons, Stephen and Lawrence, narrated with a poetic quality that has its literary equivalent in the poetic prose of the Golden Legend.

The Pauline Chapel, built by Antonio da Sangallo the Younger, under Paul III, is decorated on the side walls with two frescoes painted by Michelangelo: *The Conversion of St. Paul* (to the left coming in) and the *Crucifixion of St. Peter* (right-hand wall), the first of which was executed between 1542 and 1545, the second between 1545 and 1550. These are difficult works to grasp, full of a religious and mystic passion that finds expression with difficulty in the esthetic forms of the Renaissance. They are also very different from each other. The first is an explosion of the supernatural in the midst of nature, of the divine in the world of every day; the second is a composition that is almost coagulated, heavy and slow in the motion that seems to oppress the body but not the soul — made indomitable by faith — of the first pope.

FOREWORD TO THE VATICAN MUSEUMS

PAOLO DALLA TORRE DEL TEMPIO DI SANGUINETTO
Director General

The extraordinary complex of collections that is the Museums and Galleries of the Vatican has been studied, described and illustrated in the distinguished series on the Museums of the World, *to create a book that will be an ambassador and ideal disseminator of the results of the centuries' long high patronage of the Roman Pontiffs in the fields of history and the arts.*

From an historical point of view, it may be said that archives, libraries and museums are no more than decent, functional storehouses in which to collect, arrange, study, conserve and pass on to posterity the survivors of that perpetual shipwreck which is the past of every culture and every civilization. From the particular viewpoint of art, museums might be more properly defined as shelters for works which by the force of events and man have been torn from their original and natural surroundings.

So the specific obligation of the museum director must necessarily be that of ensuring as well as possible to the works of art in his care the repair of every degradation and disfigurement; their installation in a situation corresponding best to the lost original position for which they were commissioned and created; and their safeguarding from the inevitable perils of time. But here, in this ideal, perhaps a little Utopian museological life —which should have quiet, reasonable privacy, selective contemplation — just here is where the trouble begins. Today, with the spread of the tourist industry and the diffusion of mass-produced pseudo-culture, art is asked to run the risks of perpetual motion and to be exhibited to noisy masses of visitors and curiosity seekers. Objects and people are transported at every moment from one city to another, from one country to another, when it is not indeed from one continent to another. The works themselves no longer have any protection or peace, because of the frantic rushing back and forth to which they are subjected, and because of mania for bringing them together in one way or another — according to disparate, arbitrary and often questionable criteria — for various local, national and international exhibitions. What is more, at home or abroad, art is obliged to expose and make a questionable spectacle of itself for the enjoyment of crowds which are, to say the least, indiscreet in their dangerous effusions of admiration.

These are perplexing problems for those of us who have the difficult task of watching over the safety of inestimable treasures of the course of civilization, and at the same time of responding to the rightful imperatives of a cultural training and evolution that still must expand to include all the social strata.

A good part of the problem, it seems to us, springs from a peculiar mentality, from a sort of modern tribal idolatry, which in art is directed exclusively toward an admiration of the "original," however it may be and even if only fleetingly visible, whereas people in the past more wisely — once a real "masterpiece" had been universally recognized and acclaimed — had no difficulty at all, in fact yearned to enjoy it intellectually and lovingly from close by, in careful "copies." There is, in other words, a clear divergence between the wise old preference for a good copy of an authentic masterpiece over a doubtful original, and the unconsidered modern habit of disdaining a copy and wanting at any cost to possess, or to be able to say that one has seen, an original, even only once and hastily, no matter what it was.

(*It may be added parenthetically that this concept perhaps is not among the least causes of the present crisis in modern art.*)

That is why, confronted by the great progress in the techniques of illustration and enlightened enterprise in publishing, as in this series, it seems to us more than obvious, indeed particularly suitable, to conclude with the hope that through the increase in just such initiatives aimed at the faithful reproduction of excellent "prototypes," we shall finally reach a solution: that is, the goal of mediating seriously between the pressing need for wider knowledge and more exact study of the masterpieces of art, and the no less needed and necessary care and precautions to be exercised for the safeguarding of this heritage.

GREGORIAN–ETRUSCAN MUSEUM
PIO–CLEMENTINO MUSEUM
CHIARAMONTI MUSEUM

ORIENTALIZING ETRUSCAN ART. *Large Fibula.*

Discovered intact by the archpriest Regolini and a General Galassi in 1836, the Regolini-Galassi Tomb yielded the greatest selection of Etruscan jewelry ever recovered, and it was this find that revealed to scholars the existence of an "Orientalizing" culture. The fibula under consideration (of exceptional size as well as unusual form) is considered, on the basis of sound evidence, to be the product of a local workshop at Caere. This does not mean that the craftsmen were necessarily native Etruscans.

The technical perfection of the work is outstanding, particularly when the decoration of the "bow" (the lower curved element) of the fibula is considered. Here 55 minute figures of geese have been applied to it (obtained it is said by stamping the figures out of rolled gold and soldering them to the mount), arranged in seven rows alternating with other rows of winged lions, barely apparent in the shallow projection of the relief. This is a stylistic device presumably first "institutionalized" in Assyrian stone sculpture, but also connected with the technique of repoussé relief.

ETRUSCAN ART OF THE ARCHAIC PERIOD. *Terra-cotta Acroterion.*

The Pegasus in terra cotta (whose visible wing has been incorporated for greater firmness in the compact structure of its base) was the left-hand acroterion above the pediment of a temple in ancient Caere. To be dated at the

EXEKIAS
Black-Figure Amphora with Achilles and Ajax Playing Dice
Circa 530 B.C.
Terra cotta painted in the black-figure technique (the field left in the natural color of the clay). Details engraved with burin. Touched up with brown, white (these retouches have disappeared) and violet; height 24".
Gregorian-Etruscan Museum

beginning of the 5th century B.C. and stylistically not readily distinguishable from parallel Greek and Italiot production, it succeeds in fusing into a single coherent statement its fundamental naturalistic intention (in the spirited modeling of the head) with the radical stylization — hereditary and "canonical" — of the decorative parts and the pictorial decoration.

In particular it should be noted how the naturalistic curves which outline the nape of the animal's neck make up a "system" with the abstract development of the wing, stylized in accordance with the ancient Ionic model; and how in this complex play of curves, differing in radius and direction, the mane, the feathers and the "scales" which have been painted in, are all also involved.

EXEKIAS. *Black-Figure Amphora.*

Exekias, whose signature recurs 11 times on examples which are among the most beautiful products of Attic black-figure pottery, in only two cases (the amphora considered here and the one in Berlin with *Heracles and the Nemean Lion*) did he care to specify that he was also responsible for the pictorial decoration. On the lip of this amphora may be read in fact: *Echsekias egrapsen kapoeseme* = "Exekias painted me and made me" — instead of the usual "Exekias made me," which qualified him as a potter and which is repeated on the shoulder of the vase above the back of Archilles.

In one of the two large metope compositions (which in fact constitute the pictorial decoration of the vase, otherwise covered almost entirely with black varnish) appear the figures of Achilles (to the left) and Ajax (to the right) intent on a game of dice or checkers. From the mouths of the two

EXEKIAS
Black-Figure Amphora with the Departure (?) of the Dioscuri
(Opposite face of the same amphora.)

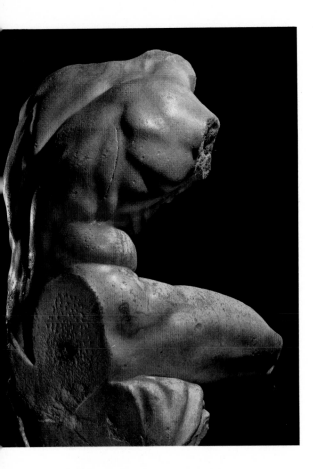

APOLLONIUS OF ATHENS
Male Torso, called the Belvedere Torso
1st century B.C.
Marble; height 62 1/2″.
Pio-Clementino Museum

heroes emerge "balloons" with their respective statements: "four" (*tesara*) on Achilles' part; "three" (*tria*) on the part of Ajax. And here the "backwards" writing assures us that the word is really coming out of his mouth. It is thus likely that the game is a kind of *Morra*, or fingers' game (with or without dice) and it is not a foregone conclusion that Ajax is losing just because he states that he has a lower number.

On the other metope are seen Pollux (with the dog) and Castor with the horse Kylaros, fêted (it is not clear whether the scene is of a return or a farewell) by Leda and Tyndareos. All are identified by their respective names. Nor is there lacking (written backwards under the belly of the horse) the inscription praising the young boy, Onetoride, who is greeted in other vases by Exekias as well, with the title of *kalòs* (beautiful), customary in such inscriptions. The Vatican amphora is the best known work by the master, who represents the ultimate and most refined phase of Attic black-figure ware. The ornamental and miniaturistic calligraphy of a Klitias, the strict compositional wisdom of an "Amasis painter" here appear perfected, while the spirit of rising naturalism and the influence of contemporary sculpture confer a new heroic dignity and a monumentality on the human figures.

The years around 530 B.C. were crucial. Around that time the new red-figure technique was born (and adapted to fully pictorial effects, as the brush was more manageable than the burin) and in the same period appeared (as documents and the work of a Cimon of Cleonae attest) the first attempts to represent oblique images in painting (foreshortenings by which shields and wheels were no longer drawn as round but as oval). These attempts were decidedly revolutionary vis-à-vis the black-figure tradition.

On the other hand, the punctilious technique of incising was utilized for calligraphic involvements making a gratuitous arabesque (although the spirals on the thighs of the players are justified by the presumable presence of metal thigh-pieces), along with certain pictorial effects of light or texture (as in the luminous Tintoretto-like construction of Achilles' foot). Thus at this point the black-figure style still succeeded in reconciling the divergent decorative and illustrative aims by which it was imbued from the beginning — but only when it was sustained by a virtuoso of the burin like Exekias.

APOLLONIUS OF ATHENS. *Male Torso Called the "Belvedere Torso."*
Of uncertain provenance (but certainly Roman), formerly in Palazzo Colonna from 1433, in the Vatican from 1523–1534 and there very much admired by artists and particularly by Michelangelo, the torso was named the *Belvedere Torso* after its previous place in the Vatican collections. It is one of the few marbles to have escaped the dangerous and often fanciful "completions" by restorers who from the Renaissance on falsified masterpieces found in fragmentary condition, until 19th-century historicism created greater respect for originals.

Nevertheless it cannot be excluded that a "modern" polishing has touched up the surfaces, which appear to be less worn than is generally the case in finds from excavations. The damage from this alteration of the surfaces is largely made up for by the recovery of the original conditions in terms of

APOLLONIUS OF ATHENS
Belvedere Torso
Front view.

what Alberti would have called the "reception of the lights." In fact the *Seated Boxer* of the Museo delle Terme — which is signed by the same Apollonius, son of Nestor, of Athens, who carved his name on the rocky base of the Vatican torso — although it is undamaged allows only an approximate appreciation of its original values. The thick accumulation verdigris, opaque and relatively light, just where the forms recede into shadow, has in places inverted the chiaroscuro relationships, which fundamentally represent the only specific reality of a sculptural work. The *Belvedere Torso* thus *is* and does not *seem to be* a masterpiece, and Apollonius turns out to be a personality of outstanding stature, even if the *Boxer* seems to reduce him. It appears that Apollonius lived in the second half of the 1st century B.C., and it is understood that he "copied" preceding works, of the 3rd and 2nd century, in the tradition of Lysippus, assuming that a neo-Attic label, in the classicist sense, has been attached to the Augustan Age, and assuming that in general, so far as late Hellenism is concerned, sculpture turned to the conception of a single viewpoint. None of this has been proved, and it is possible that the *Belvedere Torso* represents a current that on its own went beyond the results of Middle Hellenistic sculpture, that is, it took complete possession of three dimensional space and has its hallmark in torsion and spiraling movement. In this sense the *Belvedere Torso* was indeed exemplary for Michelangelo, not only in torsion and *contrapposto* but also in the emphatic anatomy of the large and compact muscular masses, which are not inert but "in action." Both the back view (p. 22) as the front view (p. 23) find exact counterparts in Michelangelo, and this, strange to say, is better seen in the pictorial than the sculptural work: from the *Ignudi* of the Sistine Ceiling, to the St. Bartholomew of the *Last Judgment*. Seated on an animal skin, the *Belvedere Torso* has been taken for the fragment of a Heracles, a Polyphemus, Prometheus, Mars, Amicus, Silenus or a Philoctetes. It is not possible to visualize, without imagining them made up with Michelangelesque replacements (certainly irrelevant), how the missing portions must have appeared (it is obvious that the work of art, if truly such, is unpredictable); and to console us we have been told that it is beautiful because it is a fragment, and entire it would be ugly.

ROMAN COPY AFTER PRAXITELES. *Venus of Cnidus.*

The *Aphrodite* or *Venus of Cnidus,* represented nude as she goes into or comes out of the bath, was the masterpiece of Praxiteles' maturity (he had the beautiful Phryne as model) and was perhaps the most famous and most imitated statue of antiquity. The Cnidians paid it homage by reproducing it on their coins in late Imperial times. From these coinages we have learned what the type and pose of the statue were, and have thus been able to recognize among the innumerable *Venuses* existing, the many that seem to be faithfully copied or derived from the *Cnidian.*

The one in the Vatican, formerly in the Colonna collection, has been restored in the neck, the left arm and the right forearm (with the "hooked" hand, invented by a Counter-Reformation restorer, that held the edge of a lead drapery, painted white — removed only in recent times — with which her nudity was partially covered before displaying her in the Vatican). The head is ancient and is also a copy of the *Cnidian,* but not related to this particular body.

ROMAN COPY AFTER PRAXITELES
Venus of Cnidus
The original, circa 350 B.C.
The copy, 1st–2nd century A.D.
Detail of the face.
Marble; height 6′, 9″.
Pio-Clementino Museum

ROMAN COPY AFTER PRAXITELES
Venus of Cnidus
Full view of statue

The Vatican *Venus* has in reality preserved little more than the general scheme of the original: the soft and discreet sinuousness of the axis of the figure, naturalistically responding to the law of gravity; and despite the artisan carving of the beautiful regular head it retains at least the echo of an expression that was originally tender and pensive — the "humid" glance praised by the ancients.

ROMAN ART — APOLLO BELVEDERE. *Re-elaboration of a 4th Century B.C. Original.*

Discovered in the 16th century on one of the Della Rovere properties (near Anzio?) and brought to the Vatican by Julius II, the *Apollo Belvedere* was restored (like the *Laocoön*) by Montorsoli, who added the missing parts (removed again a little before the second World War).

The highpoint of its popularity came with Neo-Classicism, after Winckelmann had extolled it beyond any other ancient or modern work, in a famous passage: "I place at the feet of this statue the idea of it that I have given, imitating those who placed at the feet of the simulacra of the gods the wreaths that they could not place on their heads." The *Apollo Belvedere* thus became the summit touched by Greek art in giving form to that ideal beauty which, it was considered, Phidias himself had pursued.

In reality the *Apollo* responded much more to the inclination of 17th- and 18th-century classicism than to that of the age of Pericles; it was imitated for example by Bernini, not by Michelangelo. The svelte and elegant pose of the figure, the lightness of its step, the tricky virtuoso modeling which passes from the smooth softness of the skin to the serpentine light and dark tangle of the hair, the very unusualness of the piece (which makes comparisons difficult) take us back to the "invention" of a great master. But despite the "Homeric" suggestion that flows from the image of the god "who shoots his arrows from afar" it does not seem in any way possible to go back further than the age of Alexander — when the painter Apelles discovered the category of *grace* "by which art alone succeeds in touching heaven." The Attic sculptor Leochares, who worked with Scopas and Lysippus, has been mentioned as its possible attribution, and this official hypothesis may be maintained, though with some doubt. But the style of the *Apollo* does not appear to be too far from what we know about the style of Leochares.

ROMAN IMPERIAL ART. *Sleeping Ariadne.* pp. 28–29

Acquired for the papal collection in 1512 and thought to be a Cleopatra, the Vatican *Ariadne* is an estimable Roman copy of a Middle Hellenistic (3rd–2nd century B.C.) work, inspired in its turn by the Phidian prototypes of the east pediment of the Parthenon. The rocky bed, the right hand and part of the face have been restored. The heavy sleep of the abandoned girl (who will be awakened by the arrival of Dionysus: myth of death and resurrection) is here not just an occasion for a gratuitous formalistic exhibition. And it is probable that the symbolic and dramatic content of the mythical event did not elude Michelangelo (even though he believed it to be Cleopatra), in his *Night* and *Dawn* he adopted to some extent its heavy and contorted pose and the wheeling of the arms around the head.

ROMAN COPY AFTER DOIDALSES. *Bathing Venus.*

It is from a famous *Crouching Venus* by the Bithynian artist, Doidalses, who lived in the 3rd century B.C. (the lost original was in bronze and could be seen in Rome at the time of Pliny), that the numerous examples existing today are thought to be derived. These however differ too much from one another to offer certain evidence as to the exact appearance of the original.

From it however surely derives the knowledgeable spatial construction of this figure, winding upon itself in accordance with a complex "closed form" module. The classicistic type of the head would suggest on the other hand a variation on the part of the copyist, given that the less idealized and saucier head (less "Greek" and more "French") seen in some of the other copies corresponds better to the frankly amorous and provocative charms of the nude.

ROMAN COPY (AFTER GREEK ORIGINAL). *Daughter of Niobe.*

The dramatic theme of the slaughter of the children of Niobe was tackled very early in Greek art, both in painting and sculpture. A version with many figures (disposed — it seems — in the open, as in a landscape painting) was seen by Pliny in Rome by the Temple of Apollo Sosianus (constructed in 32 B.C.). There was some doubt then whether the author was Scopas or Praxiteles. From this it appears that Pliny's attribution was stylistic (evidently a practice to which the connoisseurs of the time were already dedicated), and it was obviously justified by the simultaneous presence of Scopatian and Praxitelean motives. And this would indicate a later, already substantially "Hellenistic" moment. The group must have been copied many times: an almost complete series of the figures now in the Uffizi, in Florence, was excavated in Rome at the end of the 16th century. *The Chiaramonti Daughter of Niobe* (so named because it was originally exhibited in the rooms arranged by Pius VII under the name of Museo Chiaramonti; since 1947 it is in the Belvedere) which was discovered at Tivoli also in the 16th century and transferred to the Vatican by Cardinal Ippolite d'Este (nephew of the protector of Ariosto of the same name), repeats one of the figures of the series in Florence, but reveals a better hand (or greater fidelity to the original) in the freer treatment of the heavy drapery that corresponds to the movement of the figure, and has been given a better rhythm and more coherent stylization. Schefold, on the basis of the Florentine example (in which the head has been preserved), believes he has identified the original (lost) head of *The Chiaramonti Daughter of Niobe* in a modern bronze cast in a private Swiss collection.

EASTERN ROMAN ART. *Sarcophagus of St. Helena.* *p. 32*

Prepared for an unidentified emperor (presumably Constantius Chlorus, father of Constantine), the porphyry sarcophagus with battle scenes held the remains of St. Helena (mother of Constantine) in the mausoleum at Tor Pignattara on the Via Labicana. It was re-employed for Pope Anastasius IV (at the Lateran), and was damaged by fire in 1308. In the 18th century, in a radical restoration, many of the heads were redone; it was then given a high polish and was displayed next to the similar *Sarcophagus of Constantia*. The war scenes (Roman horsemen galloping, and felled or chained Barbarians) may call to mind the *decursio* on the Antoninus Pius

ROMAN COPY AFTER A BRONZE ORIGINAL BY THE BITHYNIAN ARTIST DOIDALSES
Bathing Venus
After a 3rd-century B.C. original.
Marble; height 32 1/4".
Pio-Clementino Museum

ROMAN COPY AFTER A GREEK OR HELLENISTIC ORIGINAL
The Chiaramonti Daughter of Niobe
1st–2nd century A.D.
(after original of 4th–3rd century B.C.)
Marble.
Chiaramonti Museum

EASTERN ROMAN ART
Sarcophagus of St. Helena
Beginning (?) of 4th century A.D.
Porphyry; height 7', 11 1/4";
length 8', 9 1/2"; width 6'.
Pio-Clementino Museum

column base in the Cortile della Pigna: a composition that is laboredly academic if compared to the bursting plastic vitality on the fronts of the most significant sarcophagi of the 3rd century. But the classicistic principle of the isolation of the figures and at the same time their emergence from the background is not to be understood here so much in terms of a traditionalist ideal of the Alexandrian milieu from which the sarcophagus presumably came, as a changed stylistic intention tending toward the decorative.

EASTERN ROMAN ART. *Sarcophagus of Constantia.*
From the Mausoleo di S. Constanza on the Via Nomentana, which was erected — apparently by Constantia (daughter of Constantine the Great) — originally to serve as a baptistry; it was employed to contain her remains when, on the death of the founder (354), the building was transformed into a mausoleum. The Diocletian period has been mentioned in connection with the sarcophagus because of the close analogies in form and style it shows with that of St. Helena, which has been supposed to date from that time. It is not very likely, however, that Constantia's body was placed in a tomb that had been carved half a century earlier. This is all the more unlikely as the motives of the grape-gathering putti, the peacocks (not visible in the photograph), the lamb — even if they may all be traceable to pagan prototypes — would not readily be found all together unless there were an explicit intention to convey a Christian meaning. It is thus more probable that both the sarcophagi go back to the age of Constantine, perhaps ordered by Constantine for himself — independent of any mournful contingency.

EASTERN ROMAN ART
Sarcophagus of Constantia
First half of 4th century A.D.
Detail. Porphyry; height 7', 4 1/2";
length 7', 8"; width 5', 1".
Pio-Clementino Museum

ROMAN ART.   *Bust of the Emperor Philip the Arabian.*

Found in the 16th century near Tor Paternò and formerly the property of Prince Chigi, the large portrait *Bust of Philip the Arabian* is part of the collection arranged by Pius VII, called the Museo Chiaramonti. The emperor is wearing the *toga contabulata* (whose rich fullness, accordion pleated and sharply ironed by pressing between two boards, creates the typical smooth band worn obliquely across the breast) and looks straight front with an absorbed and poignant expression.

Although moving from a realistic, substantially anti-classical, impulse, the author of this bust appears to be concerned less with an exact reproduction of physical features than with giving us a moral portrait of a complicated and tormented personality.

It was the lot of Philip, son of a sheik of the Hauran and first Christian emperor, to eliminate his predecessor, Gordian III, and to decree his apotheosis, to celebrate (in 248) the millennial anniversary of Rome and to die immediately afterward in battle against Decius.

ROMAN ART
*Bust of the Emperor Philip
the Arabian*
244–249 A.D.
Marble.
Chiaramonti Museum

AUGUSTAN ROMAN ART
Augustus from Prima Porta
Shortly after 20 B.C.
Figure wearing breast-plate.
Marble with traces of polychrome;
height 6', 8 1/4".
New Wing, Chiaramonti Museum

AUGUSTAN ROMAN ART. *Augustus from Prima Porta.*

Discovered in 1863 in Livia's villa *ad Gallinas Albas* at Prima Porta, the exceptionally well preserved statue of Augustus wearing a breast-plate is one of the most admired pieces in the Braccio Nuovo (New Wing). The work may be dated with relative facility from the armor. The breast-plate is of the "anatomical" or form-fitting type, and simulates the kind of decoration in which the figures are cast separately and then applied to the ground. The figures have a clear allegorical meaning: at the center a Parthian is represented in the act of returning a standard — one of the eagles taken from Crassus in 53 B.C. and recovered in 20 B.C. With the *Augustus from Prima Porta* the military iconography of the emperor (shown as a general addressing his troops) is established and remains unchanged up to and beyond Honorius. It is more difficult however to retrace "upstream" the separate cultural and stylistic components that went to make it up. The foundation, however, is substantially neo-Attic (the stance recalls, besides the *Etruscan Orator,* the *Doryphorus* of Polyclitus; and the superb idealization of the individual features has very little relationship to Republican realism, recalling more the portraiture of the Diadochi).

AGESANDER, POLYDORUS AND ATHENODORUS. *Laocoön.* *p. 36*

The *Laocoön* was discovered on January 14, 1506 in the course of a casual excavation in the vineyard of one Felice Fredi at "Sette Sale" on the Esquiline hill in Rome. Among those who gathered at the news of the find, it seems that Giuliano da Sangallo was the first to recognize the work as the one that Pliny preferred to every other sculpture or painting, and that had been carved by the Rhodian sculptors, Agesander, Polydorus and Athenodorus.

Julius II transferred the group to the Belvedere. Here it was recomposed, for it was in pieces, and then Giovanni Angelo da Montorsoli redid the missing parts in terra cotta. With respect to the present composition (restored by F. Magi, 1960) the figure of the elder son was turned some 15 degrees to the right, which gave the whole group a much more frontal and centrifugal aspect (the missing arms were redone in fully extended position), thus implying a substantially relief-type or single-view composition. Thus recomposed, the *Laocoön* had the admiration of the Renaissance, of Goethe and of Lessing, who chose the comparison with the corresponding episode in Virgil as the theme of his essay on the limits of the arts, which he titled *Laocoön.* But in 1906 Pollak found the original arm of the old man, and this was reattached in the last restoration of the group, when at the same time Montorsoli's additions were removed. Because of intrinsic evidence and the close analogies with the fragments signed by the same Rhodian artists which were recently found at Sperlonga, the group should be classed not far in time from the great frieze of Pergamon, whose extraordinary intensity of pathos it repeats (if indeed it does not anticipate). Thus the date indicated would be the 2nd century B.C. or the beginning of the 1st, at the outside. In front of the more compact and closed organic quality of the newly reorganized composition, the old suspicion is dissipated that one might be standing before a group of empty gesticulation and bombastic technical virtuosity.

On page 36:
AGESANDER, POLYDORUS AND ATHENODORUS OF RHODES
Laocoön and His Sons Assailed by Serpents
2nd–1st century B.C.
Marble; height (of Montorsoli restoration) 7', 11 1/4".
Pio-Clementino Museum

ROMAN–HELLENISTIC ART. *Ulysses in the Land of the Dead — Ulysses in the Land of the Laestrygones.*

The *Esquiline Landscapes* were discovered on April 7, 1848 during an excavation being carried out for the municipality of Rome in the old Via Graziosa (where the present Via Cavour runs), and half was recovered before and half after the short-lived Roman Republic of '49. They aroused the enthusiasm of their discoverers because of their unusualness and their excellent state of preservation, and were given to Pius IX in 1852 after having been detached from the walls on which they were painted and "judiciously" restored by a painter who is otherwise unknown.

There are seven and a half rectangular compositions (another half-panel is today in the Museo delle Terme) and all represent scenes from Ulysses' wanderings, a theme which Vitruvius had mentioned as among the subjects preferred by preceding generations for home decoration. And this is the most substantial cycle of landscape painting (rather landscape with figures) that has come down to us, and the only one that is certainly connected with Hellenistic landscape as it had been developing before the Augustan age. While admitting allegories and personifications (the identification of places can, for example, be made by the presence of the figure of the *genius loci* with his name written beside him), it is a kind of painting which is distinguished by an exceptional ability to render space naturalistically.

In the first scene — of the two showing *Ulysses in the Land of the Dead* — the seacoast moving away as far as the horizon and the progressive scaling

ROMAN–HELLENISTIC ART
Ulysses in the Land of the Laestrygones
From the *Odyssey Landscapes* series,
found on the Esquiline.

ROMAN–HELLENISTIC ART
Ulysses in the Land of the Dead
1st century B.C.
Fresco (or encaustic) on wall;
height, 59".
From the *Odyssey Landscapes* series,
found on the Esquiline.

down of the figures, seems to go back to a prototype constructed in perspective, in which the rocky bastions would have been raised on the guide lines of a squared-off ground plan previously put into a perspective that would also provide the coordinates for the scale of heights of the figures (scaled in fact to five different heights). In the second scene (a fragment), the bold foreshortening of the giant Tityus should be noted.

The other scene (p. 39) concerns Ulysses' adventure among the Laestrygones (*Idyllic Landscape* to the left, *Laestrygones Attacking* to the right); notice in particular how the alpine landscape fades into the distance with aerial perspective effects, while the perspective lines of the towers on the crest seem to vanish toward the same horizon line.

The representation of the *Attack* continues in the successive panels (now considerably diminished in effect from over-cleaning), and there is the constant practice of "annexing" a part of the next composition. Accordingly, the continuous style has been mentioned as applying here, and even a derivation from the rotolus or illuminated *volumen* (like the Japanese *makemono*) has been suggested.

LATE ATTIC ART OF THE JULIAN–CLAUDIAN PERIOD
The Aldobrandini Wedding
First half of the 1st century B.C.
Fresco painting;
height 3'; length 7', 11 1/4".

LATE ATTIC ART OF THE JULIAN–CLAUDIAN PERIOD — *Fresco of the Aldobrandini Wedding.*

The *Aldobrandini Wedding,* an ancient fresco discovered in 1605 on the Esquiline, was detached and preserved until 1818 in the Aldobrandini garden at Magnanapoli, Rome. It was long held to be (though without any foundation) a copy or derivation from a painting by Aetion representing the *Marriage of Alexander and Roxane,* described by Lucian. But in fact it deals with a nuptial allegory, and in the center may be seen the usual motive of the goddess Peitho ("Persuasion"), intent on conquering the reluctance of the hooded bride. The youth crowned with ivy (?) might be Hymen. The composition has a frieze rather than panel format, with a good rhythm and organization on the surface, but without much consistence spatially (the architectural "wings" are disposed in a way very similar to such devices in late Attic reliefs). The figures on the left are too repainted to permit useful study, but the details of the Peitho group and of the presumed Hymen show the lively fluency of the brush strokes and the robust plastic range of the hatched chiaroscuro.

Another learned interpretation has it that the mystic marriage of Bacchus

and Ariadne is represented here, but this is a hypothesis which cannot be proved or disproved on the basis of iconographic elements. Besides, in cases of this sort the exact identification of the subject would be of doubtful assistance in understanding the text. There would be the risk if anything of inducing us to seek certain notes of expression or character (the "shyness" in the face of the bride, the "Bacchic furor" in the figure of the wreathed youth, and so on) that are entirely absent from this noble stylistic and compositional exercise, whose value is predominantly historical. For the *Aldobrandini Wedding* during two centuries (until the discovery of Pompeii and Herculaneum) was almost the only available document (that was not a grotesque) of ancient painting: hence it was the obligatory point of reference for the classicism of the 17th and 18th centuries.

LATE ANTIQUE MINIATURE PAINTER
Aeneas' Ship in the Tempest
First half of the 5th century A.D.
Tempera on parchment;
height 8 3/4"; width 9".
From the so-called *Roman Virgil*.

LATE ANTIQUE MINIATURE PAINTER.   *Aeneas' Ship in the Tempest — Shepherds — From the Roman Virgil.*

The so-called Roman Virgil consists of 309 leaves, the remains of a codex that originally included the *Aeneid,* the *Bucolics* and the *Georgics.* Parts of all three of the works have survived with numerous miniatures of various formats inserted into the text. Written in "book capitals," it has been dated around the first half of the 5th century A.D., and is one of the most ancient monuments of Western book illustration. The product of a popular or provincial workshop, even where it re-elaborates older compositions it shows a lively taste for doll-like figures that border on caricature. A sense of space was completely unknown to the master of this codex. Thus, alongside of compositions such as the one showing Aeneas' ships in the tempest, that somehow hark back to the Virgilian tradition and preserve in the representation of the ships in their setting a distant memory of naturalistic syntax, we find (as in the pastoral scene) compositions entirely without any sense of environment, in which the figures of the shepherds and the animals stand out scattered against an abstract background that if anything recalls the carpet-like compositions of the floor mosaics. Nevertheless, even with his rudimentary means, the artist succeeds in giving his figures an extraordinary pictorial vivacity, which is shown as much in the elementary and effective gesticulation of the protagonists of the tempest as in the tender idyll of the mare and its foal in the pastoral scene.

LATE ANTIQUE MINIATURE PAINTER
Shepherds
First half of the 5th century A.D.
Tempera on parchment;
height 8 1/2″; width 8 3/4″
From the so-called *Roman Virgil.*

LATE ANTIQUE MINIATURE PAINTER. *Death of Dido — Building of Carthage — From the Vatican Virgil.*   *pp. 46–47*

The 75 surviving leaves of an ancient Virgilian codex, which today comprise the so-called *Vatican Virgil,* contain only a part of the *Aeneid* and the *Georgics.* The 50 miniatures preserved in the manuscript appear to be by different hands, though in the same style. The *Vatican Virgil* is our most precious remaining evidence of what Roman book illustration in the Hellenistic tradition was like.

As against the *Roman Virgil,* which in its uninhibited popular vein is in certain respects already medieval, the *Vatican Virgil* — although more or less of the same date — is part of a cultivated current for which the desire for realism (in the sense of "Pompeiian impressionism") is still alive and operative, with all the implications of corporeal quality in the figures and the "habitability" of the space. Miniatures of this period and in this style must have still been preserved in large numbers in the monastic libraries of the early Middle Ages. In fact it would not be credible that this volume by itself could have stimulated the re-appearance, though ephemeral, of naturalistic and classic impulses in Carolingian and Ottonian miniature painting. Yet today it would be difficult to find precedents more fitting either for the milieu constructed in "perspective" that unexpectedly appears in a leaf (*Pentecost*) of the *Bible of Alcuin* (9th century), or for the poignant expressionism of the bereaved mothers in the *Massacre of the Innocents*

DIXERATADQ·ILLAMEDININTERIALLATERAQ
CONLABSAMIASTICIUNICOMBISENSEMQUICAUOAI·
SCUMANTEAISCARSASQUEMANUSTICIAMORADAITA
AIRIACONEOUSSAMBACCHAIURIAMATERUEBEAI·
AMENTISCIAMUUQ·ITTEMINIOUIUIATU·

LATE ANTIQUE MINIATURE PAINTER
Death of Dido
4th–5th century A.D.
Tempera on parchment;
height 4 1/2″; width 6 1/4″.
From the *Vatican Virgil*.

painted in one of the Ottonian *scriptoria* by the master of the *Registrum Gregorii* in the famous *Codex Egberti* of Trier (10th century).

It appears that Raphael looked at the *Vatican Virgil* with interest, and someone has recently advanced the hypothesis that the spatial investigations first carried out by Giotto (in the late Pompeiian style that takes its name from the Isaac Master) may have been suggested in some way by the "perspective" in the *Death of Dido* (or by some similar leaf preserved in Rome until the end of the 13th century).

In reality what is lacking in this "perspective" is just the certainty (which to Giotto had the greatest importance) of the relationships between the separate elements. And that frontally open door shows how reluctant the painter was to commit himself to the "construction" of space. Not that he had lost a "feeling" for it, but armed with his frank shorthand technique, it was enough for him to refer to more rigorous prototypes and, without analyzing their structure, conjure up their general appearance.

Furthermore the figures stand out distinctly and plausibly in the room, have their feet solidly on the ground, and in their spirited carriage and the proud air of their heads, they show that they are living out their own drama with a vivacity that is rarely seen in contemporary wall painting, and reveals the

LATE ANTIQUE MINIATURE PAINTER
Building of Carthage
4th–5th century A.D.
Tempera on parchment;
height 6 1/4"; width 6 1/2".
From the *Vatican Virgil.*

hand of an outstanding personality. Probably by another and lesser hand is the other scene, which shows Aeneas and Achate on top of a hill, contemplating the building of Carthage. Here the touch is more summary and schematic (so that the faces, for example, are "constructed," as often in pre-Byzantine mosaics or in the miniatures of the purple codices of the 6th century, with a few juxtaposed strokes of light and dark), but the sense of space and landscape, the movement into the distance of the buildings, the greenish plain that fades into the washed-out azure of the sea and the luminous mistiness of the sky, are still admirable.

47

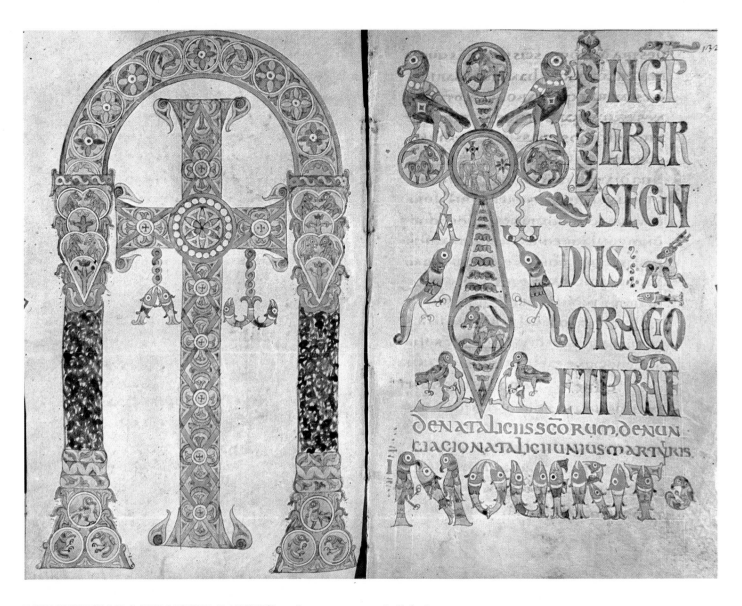

MEROVINGIAN MINIATURE PAINTER. *Sacramentary of Gelasius.*
The *Sacramentary of Gelasius* in the Vatican Library is one of the most representative examples of the singular book ornamentation that had developed in Merovingian France before Carolingian imperialism opened quite different cultural horizons.

Merovingian miniature painting usually excludes the human figure and devotes itself entirely to the meticulous display of geometric, floral and above all stylized animal motives that seem to simulate jewelry done in the technique of cloisonné enamel. To explain this style, it has been argued that a submerged Celtic strain reappeared under the pull of the animal styles of the Germanic populations, while for the motive of the letters stylized in the form of fish, appeal has been made to a symbolic intention going back to Cassiodorus. In reality these motives, though present, do not appear to be decisive (except perhaps so far as the Barbarian enamel jewelry is concerned), whereas the comparison with certain Coptic stelae with very low relief, where even the motive of the cross under an arch appears — as seen on this page — is more productive.

MEROVINGIAN MINIATURE PAINTER
Sacramentary of Gelasius:
Incipit of Second Book.
Mid 8th century.
Tempera on parchment;
height (of each of the
two pages) 10 1/4";
width (both pages) 6 1/4".

CAROLINGIAN MINIATURE PAINTER
Page of Masks Representing a Dramatis Personae.
9th century, from a 4th century original. Tempera on parchment; miniature: 9 1/2″ by 8 1/4″.
From the *Vatican Terence.*

CAROLINGIAN MINIATURE PAINTER. *The Vatican Terence.*

The *Vatican Terence* is dated in the 9th century, as the text is written in Carolingian miniscule. Terence was as popular as Virgil, and also never underwent eclipse in the Middle Ages. The prototypes of the miniatures that illustrate this codex certainly go back to the 4th–5th century. It consists substantially "in simple outline sketches of masked actors gesticulating with as much verve as the buffoons of the *Commedia dell'Arte"* (Réau).

The frontispieces of the separate plays, with the masks representing the *dramatis personae,* have — especially in the architectural frames — a certain plastic consistency supplied by washes of color. But the witty linear organization in the sketching of those grotesque faces reveals the Carolingian miniature painter's natural bent toward anti-classical deformation, though on the whole remaining faithful to his antique prototype. Some of these faces may recall the burning expressionism of the "wide-eyed orans," frequently seen in catacomb painting of the 4th century.

MIDDLE BYZANTINE MINIATURE PAINTER. *Joshua Roll.*

The *Joshua Roll,* a parchment band some 10 meters long, on which the deeds of Moses' successor are unfolded in the manner of a frieze, was long held to be one of the most ancient examples of illuminated illustrations of the Holy Scriptures. It was put back to at least the 6th century, as perhaps a copy of a 4th-century prototype; but lately the clearly Middle Byzantine character of the painter's hand has been recognized, for though the models were late antique they were interpreted in accordance with the elegant and distinctive modules of post-Iconoclastic art.

In the portion illustrated here, the city of Jericho is seen personified by a mourning woman with a crown of walls on her head; she has dropped her cornucopia and sits forsaken, by the collapsing battlements. Further to the right is Joshua, enthroned; then follow soldiers and scouts against a background of villages and cities (most elegant is the other urban personifica-

MIDDLE BYZANTINE
MINIATURE PAINTER
Joshua Roll
9th–10th century.
Detail.
Tempera on parchment;
length of entire roll: about 32′.

tion poised on top of a hill) treated with delicate graphic taste and a notable atmospheric sense in the terse discretion of the tints. The "perspective" of the city has a sense of space, and one might say that such a master as Vuolvinio had models of this sort in mind when he wrought the *Life of St. Ambrose* in the great silver altar of Milan.

It would perhaps be better, accordingly, to hold the date of the *Joshua Roll* firmly at the 9th century. Carolingian culture in fact seems to presuppose this very stage of Byzantine painting, whose naturalism seems very fresh, but is already second-hand and has institutionalized its mannerisms, stylistic devices and calligraphy, as in the elegant tangles of flying draperies and in the no less characteristic articulation of the knees. It would be enough, in fact, to consider this way of drawing the knee in order to realize that the miniatures of the *Joshua Roll* could not be faithful copies of late antique originals.

52

MACEDONIAN BYZANTINE MINIATURE PAINTER. *Vatican Psalter.*
In the post-Iconoclastic period, especially under the Macedonian dynasty (10th–11th century), Byzantine art knew a moment of exceptional splendor, which in miniature painting is shown specifically in the renewal of classicist ideals. This represents one of the most influential precedents for the successive Hellenistic revivals in the wall painting and mosaic art of the Comnenian and Paleologan ages.

Among the liturgical books, particular consideration was given to the *Book of Psalms,* and the psalters of this period can be divided into two clearly separate types: the imperial (or aristocratic) and the more modest monastic psalters. In the first group, characterized by the sumptuous charm of the large full-page miniatures, painted in gorgeous colors, often on a gold ground and splendidly framed, a highly important place (next to the superb example in Bibliothèque Nationale, Paris) goes to the 10th century *Psalter* in the Vatican. The page illustrated, with David between the figures of Wisdom and Prophecy, gives an idea of the style of these works. The backward looking inspiration, which harks back to the Hellenistic root of Byzantine representation more than to Early Christian models, seems to rely on prototypes of the Justinian age that are courtly and sacral in their stylization. One may think — in connection with the figure of David — of Justinian in the S. Vitale mosaic, as well as of the figures "in majesty" of the purple codices of the 6th century, such as the Rossano and the Sinope Gospels.

But the taste of the time is revealed in the calligraphic and elegant mannerisms of the drapery, which though showing some tendency to mimic the naturalism of the prototypes, in reality obey internal and abstract impulses, as seen in the leaping, zigzagging strokes. The spatial extensions of the supports in perspective are more apparent than real. And the miniature painters of this period, more concerned with the symmetry of the plane than with perspective values, readily made the lines of the lateral pedestals diverge rather than converge, with the result that they seem (but are not) arranged in accordance with a systematic principle of "inverse perspective," as suggested by Wulff, Grabar and others.

GEORGIUS BLACHERNITES. *Menologion of Basil II.*   *p. 54*
The *Menologion* (monthly ordinance) is the Byzantine liturgical book, which on the example of the fundamental collection of Simeon Metraphrastes (10th century) provides an anthology of the lives of the saints, arranged according to the calendar of the Eastern Church. The name of Synaxarion (as it is more a summary of the lives of the saints) would be more suitable than Menologion for the Vatican manuscript which the miniature painters Georgius, Mena, Nestor, Pantaleon, Michael and Simon — residents of the Blacherne quarter of Constantinople — prepared for the Emperor Basil II, signing their names in the margin of their compositions.

In its present state the work includes 430 miniatures; they do not differ greatly in style and are a bit monotonous because of the insistent recurrence of the theme of decapitation. The martyrdom of St. Hermione documents the decorative character and the refined artisan level of these compositions. Although certainly derived from prototypes that in turn hark back to antiquity (as with the *Joshua Roll*), these landscapes, with their capriciously

BYZANTINE MINIATURE PAINTER OF THE MACEDONIAN PERIOD
David Between the Personifications of Wisdom and Prophecy
10th century.
Tempera on parchment; height 13″, width 9 1/2″.
From the *Vatican Psalter.*

colored mountains painted on gold grounds, have lost any naturalistic significance. The rich live action of the brush in the gold lights and the touches of white is noteworthy, and these effects are particularly appropriate on the crests of the hills, which thus acquire an ascending rhythm as if heaped up by the movement of waves. It is a motive that will be found again in the landscapes of the Kariye Djami Church in Constantinople.

MACEDONIAN BYZANTINE MINIATURIST. *Bible of Leo the Patrician.* Aside from the *Paris* and *Vatican Psalters,* the *Bible of Leo the Patrician* is the most splendid example of the courtly type of Macedonian miniature that looks back to antiquity. The page with *Moses Receiving the Tables of the Law on Mount Sinai* refers back — in the landscape setting required by the event represented — directly to and then beyond Early Christian and Justinian suggestions, to the Pompeiian roots of landscape painting.

The precious splendor of the colors does not stifle the sense of landscape, even though it is a Surreal scene of rocks that fade into a grey and hallucinatory sky, smoking with wandering vapors (from which, plausibly, comes the Hand of God). The handling of the brush is free, fluent and accurate

GEORGIUS BLACHERNITES
Martyrdom of St. Hermione
Around the year 1000.
Tempera on parchment; height of entire page, 14 1/4";
width, 11".
From the *Menologion of Basil II.*

BYZANTINE MINIATURE PAINTER
OF THE MACEDONIAN PERIOD
Moses Receiving the Tables of the Law
10th century.
Tempera on parchment;
height 14 1/2"; width 9 3/4".
From the *Bible of Leo the Patrician.*

54

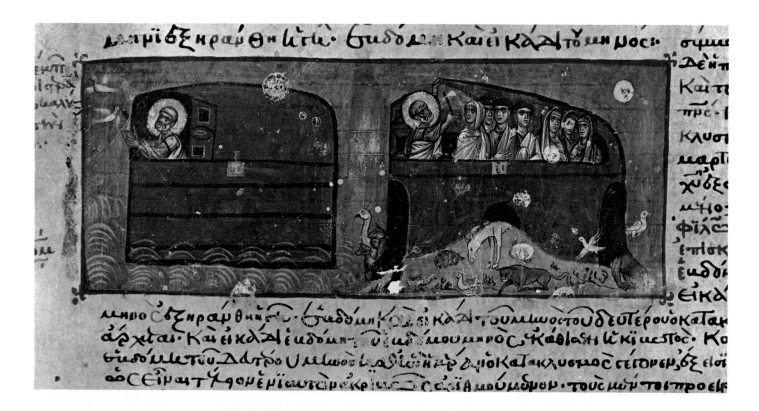

(and always obedient to a more rhythmic than "functional" dynamic impulse). The movement of the figures, drapery and heads is ably constructed with delicate but decisive touches.

From works like this, in the second half of the 13th century, will flow the Byzantinizing current of Bolognese miniature painting, which at its high point will produce the *Bibles* of Paris, Madrid, Gerona and London, and the *Psalter* of the Bologna library; and which one day will count alongside the names of a Jacopino da Reggio, a Bernardino da Modena and a Jacopo di Paolo dell'Avvocato, the more weighty names of Oderisi and of Franco.

COMNENIAN BYZANTINE MINIATURIST. *Vatican Octoteuch*
In the Byzantine world it was often the custom to make up a volume out of the first eight books of the Old Testament (the five *Books of Moses,* from *Genesis* to *Exodus,* plus the *Books of Joshua, Judges* and *Ruth*), and these collections were called octoteuchs. The *Vatican Octoteuch,* previously dated as 11th century, is today more reliably considered to be from the 12th. The courtly culture of the Macedonian psalters here seems to have met with a fresh narrative vein of a popular character. The conventionalized and canonical repertory of stylistic devices and symbols (house, tree, flowers, chairs, drapery and the formulas for the faces) is employed in a less subtle and less perfect system, but (a trifle confusedly) with much more nonchalance. It certainly cannot be said, for instance, that in the two episodes of *Noah* the story is not told with complete clarity; while in the other scene of *Abraham and Sarah Before Pharaoh* the lively participation of the figures in the action is to be noted — a scene one might say that has been relived with an earthy confidence which may recall the Little Masters of the Florentine Dugento.

56

BYZANTINE MINIATURE PAINTER
OF THE EARLY COMNENIAN PERIOD
Noah's Ark
12th century.
Tempera on parchment;
miniature: 3" × 7 1/2".
From the *Vatican Octoteuch.*

BYZANTINE MINIATURE PAINTER
OF THE EARLY COMNENIAN PERIOD
Abraham and Sarah before Pharaoh
Tempera on parchment;
miniature: 5" × 3".
Detail.
From the *Vatican Octoteuch.*

JUSTINIAN (?) BYZANTINE ART. *Annunciation.*

The fragment of silk fabric, of which a detail is shown here, originally was used to wrap some reliquary, and has been cut irregularly, probably to eliminate worn-out parts. It is possible, however, to reconstruct the design of the entire piece, which had an allover motive of interlaced circles, within which were represented alternately the *Annunciation* and the *Nativity*.

It was at first thought that the textile was of Coptic provenance, but the refined stylization and the advanced manneristic reduction of naturalistic data would lend credence to the hypothesis of a metropolitan provenance and a relatively early date ("not before the 6th century") for the fragment — a

JUSTINIAN (?) BYZANTINE ART
Annunciation
6th century.
Detail of a fragment of cloth from the Lateran treasure of the *Sancta Sanctorum.* Woven silk; total length of the piece: 27"; diameter of the circles containing the figures: 12 1/2".

period when Coptic textiles had taken another direction. It is worth considering the exact finish of the weaving, the incredible flexibility of a textile technique capable of reproducing with its own means the most subtle refinements of a freely painted study or model, in the figures as in the flowers.

PRE–ROMANESQUE ART OF LATIUM. *Rambona Diptych.*

The *Rambona Diptych* has on its front leaf the figure of the *Virgin in Majesty* above, the figures of three saints in the middle and, below, a strange winged genius. On the back leaf is the *Crucifixion,* and at its foot the *Roman She-Wolf,* derived from a variation from the Capitoline she-wolf.

As the ungrammatical inscription informs us, the work was commissioned by one Odelricus, abbot of the monastery of "Rambona" (Arabona near Tolentino, founded in 889 by Ageltruda, wife of King Guido of Spoleto). Its very crude character would seem to suggest the work of a local workshop in the decadent Rome of the 10th century. It should be noted, however, that it is not a popular work "without any style," and that the convention of the figures, in particular that of the winged genius, corresponds fairly exactly with what one sees in contemporaneous Mozarabic illumination.

ROMAN–BYZANTINE ART (?)
Reliquary of the True Cross
9th century.
Gold and enamel; 10 1/2″ × 7″.
From the Lateran treasure of
the *Sancta Sanctorum*.

ROMAN–BYZANTINE ART (?).   *Reliquary of the True Cross.*

As indicated by the inscription it bears — *Pascalis episcopus fieri iussit,* meaning that it was commissioned by Bishop Paschal — the enameled cross of the Chapel of the *Sancta Sanctorum* is of the time of Pope Paschal (9th century), who also had its silver case made. The enamels that cover the cross's entire surface represent scenes from the life of Christ, from the *Annunciation* to the *Baptism,* and are very lively portrayals even in the contracted shorthand imposed by the enamel technique. The use of line — here the gold edging that separates the forms within the flat gem-like fields of color — has some relationship to contemporary Roman mosaics. There is no reason to consider the reliquary a product of artists who came from the East, as up to the 9th century Rome was in the Byzantine cultural area.

SISTINE CHAPEL
PAULINE CHAPEL

INTERIOR OF THE SISTINE CHAPEL.

The architectural plan for the building, founded in the latter half of 1473, in an advanced stage of construction in '77 and finished around 1480, is attributed by Vasari to Baccio Pontelli. Historical and stylistic considerations make this attribution probable if not certain.

The Renaissance had made "its entrance into Rome walking on Gothic crutches" (Bruhns), and while the Florentine burghers were erecting their extremely gentlemanly palaces, marked by sober decorum and clear measure, the houses of the great Roman families — a class of proud and turbulent aristocrats — in the 15th century were still being built with turrets and battlements, and closed off with high rough walls. The Sistine, too, was created not only as the "major chapel of the Sacred Palace" but also as a military redoubt of the Vatican city, which had been conceived from the time of Nicholas V as an armed citadel at the edge of the great, illustrious and untrustworthy metropolis of Rome. The idea that Sixtus IV proposed to his architect was to erect a building that on the exterior would appear as a bulwark and defence of the Church and of the supreme and absolute authority of the pontiff, and on the interior would express the conception of the firm and jealous guardianship of the purity of the Faith and the solemn manifestations of its principles. The architect was able to give concrete form to this thought by designing the exterior in the form of a high and sturdy bastion, and on the interior creating a hall notable for its simplicity and geometrical severity, and for the weighty and hermetic sealing of the space with a barrel vault carried on lunettes. In short, he defined a firmly limited interior which nevertheless gives the feeling of ample space. To "read" the interior space of the chapel correctly it is necessary to take into account both the real membering — the horizontal cornices, the upper order of pilasters, the balcony-style tribune, the marble screen — and the simulated, painted membering, such as the pilasters of the two lower orders and the niches of the popes in the upper order; for unquestionably the architecture of the chapel was conceived in conjunction with its pictorial decoration, for which the architect certainly provided the divisions and proportions. Thus the rectangular hall, divided in two by the screen and regularly measured off into rectangular fields by the painted and real pilasters, bears the impress of a quiet geometry that breathes a sense of isolation and detachment, of jealous closure and strict protection from the world. The effect naturally was more apparent when the ceiling bore only the starry-sky decoration painted by Piermatteo d'Amelia, before Michelangelo imposed on it his framework of illusionary architecture and his powerful and awesome figures. The majestic vault, originally conceived as an unbroken span for the immense, precious casket, nevertheless possessed in its brilliant connection between walls and cap-like vault an implicit dynamic content, on which without sapping it Michelangelo was able to graft the powerful tension of his framework. Even if the absolute purity of expressive creativity is lacking in the Sistine, one cannot deny the author the possession of the highest gifts as a learned practitioner of architecture, and the intelligence to have known how to translate into adequate expression the guiding idea of Pope Sixtus. This was the creation of a sacred place where intimacy of meditation would not exclude the formality necessary in the public manifestation of the sacred principles and authority of the head of the Church.

BACIO PONTELLI (?)
Florence circa 1450 — Urbino circa 1494.
Interior of the Sistine Chapel
In construction from 1472 to about 1480;
length 119', 9"; width 43', 12";
height 68'.

SANDRO BOTTICELLI. *The Temptations of Christ.*

Usually this fresco is given the title of *Purification* or the *Leper's Sacrifice,* for the scene in the foreground was interpreted by Steinmann and Horne as representing the sacrifice offered in accordance with Mosaic law by the leper after his miraculous cure. According to the recent research of Ettlinger, however, the scene shows the *Ministry of Christ in the Temple of Jerusalem,* following an apocryphal book translated and published by Filelfo, with dedication to Sixtus IV, in 1479. Thus in the context of the typological parallelism between Moses and Christ, which is the general theme of the cycle, this scene would emphasize the fact that like Moses, Jesus was also king, law-giver and priest. As the scenes of the *Three Temptations* in the background correspond in the fresco opposite to the trials undergone by Moses before receiving from Jehovah the mission of setting his people free, so the central scene of the ministry would correspond to the mission received by Moses in the scene of the Burning Bush. Despite the melodious fluency of the linear development, the lightness of the color and the picturesque view of an idyllic landscape, it must be admitted that Botticelli has not succeeded in mastering the task of creating a large composition peopled with many figures in different episodes. The relationship between the figures and the environment is neither spatial nor rhythmic, and in consequence the scenes in the background are not disposed in an order that has significance from the point of view of the compositional organization. Even the interesting and romantic interpretation of the classical motives, in the putto with the grapes and the woman carrying wood, are isolated in the dispersed context.

SANDRO BOTTICELLI
(ALESSANDRO FILIPEPI)
Florence 1445 — Florence 1510
The Temptations of Christ
1481–1482
Fresco: about 11', 4" × 18', 3".

SANDRO BOTTICELLI
The Temptations of Christ
Detail.

SANDRO BOTTICELLI
The Trials of Moses
1481–1482
Fresco: 11', 5" × 18', 4".

SANDRO BOTTICELLI
The Trials of Moses
Detail.

SANDRO BOTTICELLI. *The Trials of Moses.*

The trials are those that Moses, forced into exile in the land of Madian, underwent before being called by God to the work of redeeming his people. They are intended as parallels to the temptations of Christ, which are represented in the fresco opposite. On the right, Moses slays an Egyptian who had mistreated a Jew (being succored by a woman on the threshold of a porticoed house). Following this, in the background, is seen the flight of Moses. A little more to the left and toward the foreground, Moses confronts the shepherds who had driven away from the spring the flock belonging to the daughters of the priest, Jethro. Then, center foreground, he waters the flock in the presence of the two girls. On the left in the background, Moses removes his shoes and then kneels to hear the orders that Jehovah, who has appeared in a burning bush, will give him. In the foreground, Moses is on a journey with all of his family and his brother Aaron; perhaps the exodus from Egypt is represented. In this composition the painter manages to overcome brilliantly the difficulties offered by the complicated and dispersive theme, through his personal conception, already affirmed in the *Primavera,* by which the space is identified with the development of the action in time by means of the melodic course of the line. The unity of the composition is achieved by the insertion of the diagonal movement of the landscape into the angular and contrasted rhythm of the figures, whose tension is relaxed in the bucolic interlude of the meeting with the daughters of Jethro. It is the dominant episode, but not the absolute center of the composition, as it also is inserted into the linear development of the picture.

COSIMO ROSSELLI
Florence 1439 — Florence 1507
Moses Receiving the Tables of the Law
1481–1482
Fresco: about 11', 6" × 18'.

COSIMO ROSSELLI. *Moses Receives the Tables of the Law.*
The central theme is *Moses Receiving the Tables of the Law* (in the center, above) and the *Imposition of the Law upon the People* (left foreground), intended as a parallel to the *Sermon on the Mount.* The fresco, however, also shows us the wrath of Moses, who on descending from Sinai finds his people worshipping the Golden Calf, breaks the tables (center foreground) and orders the faithful Levites to exact an atrocious revenge on the idolators (middle ground, right). There are some uncertainties in interpretation. What is the meaning of the group in the right foreground? Does the story begin with the group of Moses on the Mount before the Lord, or below with Moses breaking the tables? Or is the scene on the Mount ambivalent, referring to the first as well as the second reception of the Law, or does it refer only to the second and definitive occasion, relegating the first ascent of Sinai to past history and silence? These doubts show that the painter did not know how to master the complicated subject matter, just as he did not know how to render the dramatic substance and the epic value of the events he was asked to illustrate. Although everything is narrated with some sense of grace, it is all monotonous. Nonetheless the impression it makes is not disagreeable; indeed the clarity of the color, animated by rich highlights, as well as the subdued and quiet rhythms, are pleasing. To explain the presence of such positive aspects in the mediocre painting of Cosimo Rosselli, it has often been conjectured that he had the benefit of Piero di Cosimo's collaboration, especially in the landscape. In reality this work represents Rosselli's own maximum effort, under the influence of Botticelli and Ghirlandajo, his greatest colleagues in the Sistine Chapel.

PERUGINO AND PINTURICCHIO. *Baptism of Christ.*
The scene is the typological parallel to the *Circumcision of the Son of Moses* in the fresco opposite. The two flanking scenes, showing *John the Baptist Preaching,* on the left, and *Jesus Preaching,* on the right, are meant to allude, according to Ettlinger, to the fullness of the work of redemption. In fact, according to Pietro Lombardo, an author favored by Pope Sixtus, whereas the baptism given by John served as a spur to repentance, the remission of sins could take place only through Christian baptism.

The fresco is identified by Vasari as the work of Perugino. Modern criticism, however, has turned toward recognizing Pinturicchio as a large participant in the work. Perugino is recognizable almost exclusively in the execution of the two main figures, drawn with ease and breadth, and of the seated nude. The latter is unquestionably the most beautiful image in the picture, in the classical sobriety of its construction, in its simplicity and vigor suffused with melancholy. If it has some accents recalling Signorelli, this is easily explained, as Signorelli was then also working in the chapel.

PERUGINO
(PIETRO VANNUCCI)
Città della Pieve 1448 —
Fontignano 1523
PINTURICCHIO
(BERNARDINO DI BETTO)
Perugia 1454 — Siena 1513
Baptism of Christ
1481–1482
Fresco: about 11', 2" × 17', 9".

As for the composition as a whole, it is doubtful whether Perugino provided the cartoon. The general layout, the type of landscape and most of the figures — at least those in the foreground — seem to belong to Pinturicchio. Although the presence of other minor collaborators is not to be excluded, it seems certain that the fine portraits in the foreground are eminent examples of the art of Pinturicchio, intent on adopting for his own, though with more delicate and lingering inflections, the sober virtues of Perugino as a portraitist. It is here that Bernardino di Betto achieves his highest results. **69**

DOMENICO GHIRLANDAJO. *The Calling of Peter and Andrew.*

GHIRLANDAJO
(DOMENICO BIGORDI)
Florence 1449 — Florence 1494
The Calling of Peter and Andrew
1481–1482
Fresco: about 11', 6" × 18'.

This corresponds to the *Crossing of the Red Sea* on the opposite wall. The parallel between the two compositions is rightly explained by Sauer in the presence of the sea in both scenes. Just as the enemies of the Faith were destroyed by the sea, so Christ calls from the sea the Apostles, who are the defenders of the Faith. Thus conceived, the parallel falls into line with the concepts that Pope Sixtus meant to proclaim from the storied walls of the chapel. Although not executed in its entirety by the master, the fresco is impressive because of the spatial breadth in the deep landscape perspective and the pictorial solidity of the groups of figures. The narrative is at the same time ornate (in the variety of the attitudes, in the variegated colors) and austere, and in this Ghirlandajo shows his grasp of the particular requirements of great dignity and calm utterance that the place to be decorated, and the nature and significance of the stories to be painted, imposed on the artists. Thus he was ready to acquire from Perugino suggestions on spatial amplitude, while at the same time — returning to Florentine tradition — he was constraining his own tendency toward picturesque illustration within forms dictated by a will to recover the archaic severity of Masaccio.

COSIMO ROSSELLI AND BIAGIO D'ANTONIO TUCCI. *The Last Supper.*

There is a clear typological parallel with the *Testament of Moses,* dedicated along the lines of Deuteronomy, to the promulgation of the Mosaic law and the transmission of the power to Joshua. The *Promulgation of the Law* corresponds here to the *Institution of the Eucharist,* that is the consecration of the beginning of the era of Grace. In the background, as if beyond a sort of loggia, are discerned the *Prayer in the Garden of Olives, The Arrest of Christ* and the *Crucifixion,* scenes — except for the second — which also find their pairs in the corresponding fresco of Moses. Vasari, always very critical in regard to Rosselli, admired in this composition the mastery shown by the painter in the perspective construction: "he did a table with eight sides drawn in perspective, and above it similarly in eight sides the ceiling, in which foreshortening very well he showed that he understood as much as the others of this art." For our part we should say that this is indeed a valuable aspect, not only as it appeared to his biographer as an exercise in technical virtuosity, but also as an appropriate means of conferring greater breadth as well as high dignity on the scene. It should be borne in mind, besides, that according to the wish of Pope Sixtus it was not a matter so much of narrating stories as of presenting the sacred events in terms of their ideological significance, which involved rendering them with a particular majestic, and in a certain sense abstract, formality. The intention was well understood by Rosselli in this case. To meet the requirement for painting that would be not only careful and honest, but also convey a consistent highly dignified tone, he knew how to hold within bounds his stylistic eclecticism, which here brings together and fuses motives borrowed from Castagno and Ghirlandajo, with Peruginian accents and even some echoes of Botticelli. It was not his son Piero who assisted the painter, as the older critics maintained, but the conjectural Utile, now certainly to be identified with Biagio D'Antonio Tucci, active in Florence and Faenza, whose hand may be distinguished in the little scenes of the *Arrest* and the *Crucifixion.*

COSIMO ROSSELLI
Florence 1439 — Florence 1507
BIAGIO D'ANTONIO TUCCI
Florence 1446 — Florence 1515
The Last Supper
1481–1482
Fresco: about 11', 6" × 18'.

70

PIETRO PERUGINO. *Christ Giving the Keys to St. Peter.*

It was given to Perugino to paint, parallel to Botticelli's *Destruction of the Company of Korah, and of the Sons of Aaron,* the fresco ideologically most important in the entire cycle: the one containing the legitimation of the absolute power of the Pope. It is a fact that in clarity of formal exposition and dignity of utterance, this composition responds better than any other to the spirit that Pope Sixtus wanted to impress on his chapel, and on the paintings that adorned it. Viewing the entire composition, we observe the complete correspondence of the style — above all in the circulating vision of space, already verging on Raphael, and governed by a radiating system of perspective lines converging on the temple — with the clarity and hierarchy of values controlling the illustrative conception. In the detail reproduced here, it is worth observing how the figures in the foreground, arranged on a sort of stage in front of the space defined by the perspective, are constructed and draped with Florentine solidity, and are animated by a breath of the vehemence of Melozzo. They live in the rarefied atmosphere created by the slow amplitude of the rhythm that links them all in turn, and by the intensely musical modulation of the volumes. With the intensity of the color and the terse luminous quality recalling Piero della Francesca, the composition seems to voice a slow, sweetly harmonious song, like a smooth and solemn sacred ceremony.

PIETRO PERUGINO
Christ Giving the Keys to St. Peter
1481–1482
Detail.
Fresco: around 11' × 18'.

PERUGINO AND PINTURICCHIO. *Circumcision of the Son of Moses.*

In this detail we discern in the background a shepherds' dance, alluding perhaps to Moses' life in the land of Madian before he was called by the Lord. In the foreground is the family of Moses setting out on their journey after having left Jethro. Perugino perhaps supplied a summary sketch of the composition, and entrusted its execution in greater part to Pinturicchio, who is called to mind by the landscape, the picturesque aspects of the narration and of the figures. Despite resemblance to the tranquil rhythms of Perugino, this style readily embraces illustrative motives, following the example of Benozzo Gozzoli's Umbrian frescoes. The critics are silent on this score, but where we would be inclined to discern the hand of Perugino is in the little scene of the dancing shepherds. Who if not the great Umbrian would have given the group such a wealth and precision of rhythmic allurements as to make this bucolic scene the liveliest part of the picture?

MICHELANGELO. *Ceiling of the Sistine Chapel.*

In 1508 Julius II decided to entrust Michelangelo Buonarroti with the complete redecoration of the ceiling, which had been frescoed as a starry firmament in 1481 by Piermatteo d'Amelia. His first program provided only for the figures of the twelve Apostles in the spandrels, and simulated coffering in the vault. The imagination of the artist, however, was still populated by the powerful images of nude slaves struggling within the blocks of marble that had been prepared for the tomb of Julius II to be erected in St. Peter's (the project had been suspended by the pope's decision to have Bramante rebuild the basilica). Michelangelo subsequently related: "I had done certain drawings, but it seemed to me to be a poor thing. Whereupon he [the pope] made me another allocution about the scenes below, and how I could do on the ceiling what I wished." In this way the present grandiose complex of representations had its origin, with the artist playing a large part in deciding on the subjects. It is indispensable to bear this in mind if one wishes to understand from its very beginnings the perfect correspondence between form and ideological content in the Sistine ceiling. Uncertain in details, the chronology is absolutely sure for the project as a whole. It is probable that Michelangelo mounted his scaffolding in August 1508 and began to work on the entrance side of the chapel, proceeding inversely in relation to the chronological sequence of the Bible stories. The first interruption, and the first removal of the scaffolding, must have taken place after the execution of the first three scenes and adjoining portions, as starting with *The Fall* the style and proportions become more ample and more suited to the distance from the spectator. A second interruption took place in August 1511, when it is attested that more than half of the ceiling, including the *Creation of Adam* and the *Creation of Eve,* was uncovered. Between September 1511 and October 1512, the remaining parts of the ceiling and the lunettes were completed. In interpreting the content of the work, modern critics have followed two opposite directions, now orienting themselves toward the ideological systems of medieval tradition, now toward the Neo-Platonic theories dear to 15th-century Florence. As Michelangelo in youth had relations with the circle of Fra Girolamo Savonarola, as well as with the humanist milieus around Lorenzo de' Medici, both directions were feasible. Nevertheless it is hard to see why Michelangelo would have been interested in conceiving the ceiling paintings as a Tree of Jesse, in the terms of the Dominican theologian, Sante Pagnini (Wind), or as the Tree of Life in the sense of St. Bonaventura and Cardinal Vigerio (Hartt). Nearer the truth would seem to be the interpretations in the Neo-Platonic key, culminating in that of Tolnay, so long as they are held to the possibilities for translation into pictorial terms that are consonant with Michelangelo's imagination. As the walls of the chapel already bore, in typological parallel, the story of mankind in the era of the Law instituted by Moses, and in that of Grace inaugurated by Christ, it was logical to devote the ceiling to the history of humanity before the appearance of the great Law-Giver, and thus to the Creation and the first events of man. To show the most ancient vicissitudes of man as already directed toward the supreme goal of redemption, the four "miraculous deliveries of Israel," prefiguring the Redemption, were frescoed in the corners of the vault; the stories from the Book of Kings, in the medallions; and above all — between the lu-

General scheme of the Sistine Chapel ceiling

On pages 76–77:
MICHELANGELO BUONARROTI
Florence 1475 — Rome 1564
The Sistine Ceiling
1508–1512
Fresco: projected on a flat surface,
119', 9" × 43' 11".
Detail.

nettes — the gigantic images of the Soothsayers — the Hebrew Prophets, who foresaw the coming of Christ, and the ancient Sibyls, who also participated, though in a shadowy way, in the presentiment of the Christian rebirth. In this way, not only was the classical world also included in the prehistory of redemption, but the civilization of antiquity was ennobled in accordance with the spirit of the Renaissance. As allusion to the humanity of the Gentiles, that is to the Greco-Roman world felt as the repository of an unsurpassed ideal of beauty (Platonically identified with the Good) are to be interpreted the mysterious nude male figures — the *Ignudi.* They may be understood as a Christian-classical synthesis of angel and Eros, but in the mind of their creator they had primarily the *expressive* function of commenting with dramatic animation on the great events of the central scenes. If the Prophets and the Sibyls represent the preparation of the redemption in the spirit, the series of Ancestors of Christ, in the spandrels and lunettes, alludes to its preparation in the body. In conclusion, and taking into account the fact that the central scenes cover the time from the *Creation* to the *Flood,* and from the reconciliation after the *Flood* up to the new fall into sin (*The Shame of Noah*), it is clear that the fundamental concept is that of man's aspiration toward redemption. This concept is expressed by Michelangelo in a grandiose vision of history, in which the religious and moral ideals of the Jewish-Christian tradition coincide with the esthetic and moral values of classical antiquity. The recognition of this coincidence in the mind of Michelangelo, as realized through the medium of Neo-Platonic thought, and the general interpretation that has been sketched above, explain the apparent contrast which strikes every observer in his first glance at the Sistine ceiling. On the one hand there is the dramatic agitation, the extraordinary animation of all the forms and all the images; on the other, the exalted, serene beauty, the solid order that checks and restricts that sublime tumult. No other theme than the aspiration toward salvation could have responded better to Michelangelo's dual moral and esthetic impulse. And the triumph of the nude in the Sistine compositions derives less from abstract formal preferences than from the veneration for antiquity understood as the spiritual meeting ground for the Good and the Beautiful. All the critics agree in considering the central scenes as visions of the Prophets and Sibyls, both because there is no perspective illusionism in their general structure, and because considering them as retrospective visions (events that have already taken place) would heighten their anagogic significance as prefigurations of the events of Redemption. But, considering that Michelangelo projected the planned sepulchral monument of Julius II onto the Sistine ceiling, we should rather see these as simulated sculpture.

Considered in themselves, however, the representations acquire a high degree of reality, appearing as figures of a transient world in passage between reality and simulation. Thus there is no reason to ascribe a lesser degree of reality to the biblical scenes than to the images of the Prophets, the Sibyls and the *Ignudi.* Indeed, if in respect to the architecture of the chapel the representations are intended as simulated sculpture, the fact is that the artist, in happy contradiction, then invests all of the reality with their plasticity. In the end it is vain to debate whether the figures are meant to be live or sculpted, since their vitality is identified with their sculptural plasticity.

75

MICHELANGELO. *Creation of Adam.*

The value of this composition in its formal and expressive aspects will not be understood completely unless one bears in mind the radical iconographic revolution accomplished by Michelangelo. Before him the Creation had been conceived as the work of a Daedalus who shapes the first man out of the mud of the earth, or as that of a thaumaturge who infuses breath into an already formed Adam by the laying on of the hand. Only Michelangelo shows us the Creator as an original force of nature. The organization of the composition around the counterpart relationship between the bare earth on which Adam lies and the wind-swollen mantle of the Lord, thus acquires full significance. Like no other artist, Michelangelo has positively rendered

MICHELANGELO
The Creation of Adam
Sixth of the biblical scenes
(counting from the entrance).
Fresco. Probably executed in the
final months of 1511.

here the terrible solemnity of the barely created world and the idea of God as absolute vital energy. The pictorial conception is of such elemental simplicity, that the felicitous invention of the vital spark struck by the contact of the fingers assumes the highest prominence. In the dialectical contrast between the spherical structure of the mantle that shelters the restless band of angels, and the elongation of the line of His body, the image of the Lord acquires human size and at the same time conveys a sense of lightning flight. The figure of Adam, on the other hand, with the robust body in balanced pose, has superb beauty in which the harmony of the form coincides with the harmony of the rhythm of the limbs, sluggish and impatient at the same time.

79

MICHELANGELO. *The Fall and Expulsion from Eden.*

The two scenes balance each other perfectly at either side of the composition, whose axis is constituted by the tree on which the serpent is wound. It is, however, a dynamic equilibrium, full of tension, as the liberation of energy seen in the bodies of Adam and Eve, pursued by the sword of the angel, seems like the natural consequence of the accumulation of compressed strength in the scene of *The Fall*, where the figures are characterized by *contrapposto*, torsion and a closed-in plastic construction. The tragedy is thus already forceful in the first scene; from this stems the pregnant sense of fatality that informs the entire composition. In the *Expulsion*, Michelangelo — who in early youth had fortified the teaching of his master, Ghirlandajo, with the study of Masaccio's frescoes — offers homage to Masaccio, whose famous paintings in the Brancacci Chapel are clearly reflected in the foreshortening of the Angel and in the springy step of the figures in flight. Yet he articulates the nudes differently, gives the relief a fuller roundness and the contours a more powerful undulation. Compared to the heroic acceptance of harsh fate found in Masaccio's composition, here the drama has become more tormented, the grief more rebellious.

MICHELANGELO. *Creation of Eve.*

In the *Creation of Eve* there is also a recollection of Masaccio: here in the scenes of the creation of man and of woman, and of mankind's first fatal steps, where the theme seemed to call for a higher simplicity, Michelangelo felt the need to turn again to the master who had inspired him at the beginning of his career with the taste for the highest moral austerity. For the figure of God the Father, enclosed in rocky drapery like the Apostles in *The Tribute Money*, Michelangelo uses one of his youthful drawings from the frescoes of the Brancacci Chapel, heightening Masaccio's heroic human quality to a superhuman *terribilità*. The tremendous power of the compact mass and the charged energy of this image is so irresistible, that the launching forth of Eve really seems the result of the magnetic force of God's gesture. In its parallelogram structure, the composition is still and compact, like a field of gravity. In simple and decisive style it expresses the feeling of dramatic destiny inherent in the very act of creation, and already advances here, as in the *Creation of Adam* and the scenes of the creation of the world, its personal, modern conception of God the Creator, and of the formation of the universe. In his anthropomorphically biblical image of the Eternal of Days, Michelangelo did not intend only to represent a sturdy old man, but wanted to invest that terrible and venerable image with an absolute cosmic force. And it is just in the fact that this unquestionably and totally human figure evokes the idea of an irresistible force, that the events of the Creation — even in the most difficult representations of the creation of the sky, the earth, the waters, light, etc. — can find not only the usual symbolic allusion but true and proper portrayal. It should be noticed that the surrounding *Ignudi* seem to derive their rhythmic excitement from the tremendous compressed and constrained forces of the central compositions.

MICHELANGELO
The Creation of Eve
The Fall and *The Expulsion from the Garden of Eden*
(fourth and fifth biblical scenes counting from the entrance).
Fresco.
The *Creation of Eve* was probably executed in the autumn of 1510; *The Fall*, about a year later, from September 1511 on.

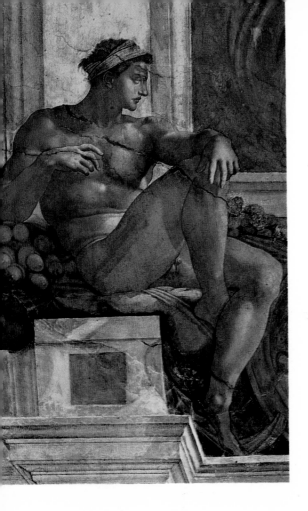

MICHELANGELO. *The* Ignudi.

It has already been suggested that the figures of the large *Ignudi* (pp. 81, 82, 83) shown on the cornice framing the smaller scenes, and supporting from above the bronze medallions bearing biblical scenes, are probably to be understood as angels who assume the classical forms of the Platonic Eros. They thus belong to those allusions to the humanity of the Gentiles, of which the Sibyls clearly are part, and accordingly to the Greco-Roman world that the artist wished to include, along with the men of the Bible, in the universal history of humanity before the Law, but already aspiring to Redemption. And it has already been said that the *Ignudi* also count as expressive elements, which is that of echoing with their exalted animation the drama taking place in the central scenes. The figure reproduced to the upper left belongs to the group following the fresco of the *Separation of the Dry Land from the Waters,* which was the first in order of execution (chronologically last) of the scenes of the creation of the word. The *Ignudi* participate in the crescendo of animation that marks the scene, as the origin of the cosmos is gradually approached. And here two of them — below left and opposite — gather their forces in masses blocked, for one thing, by the firmness of the profile, or let themselves go in free dramatic movements. Observe how in part the expressive force depends on the relationship between the intense expansion of the plastic mass and the great firmness of the contours.

MICHELANGELO
Ignudi (Male Nudes)
Flanking the scene of the *Separation of the Dry Land from the Waters.*
Frescoes probably executed in 1512.

MICHELANGELO. *The Flood.* set. 84

In order of execution this is among the earliest parts of the ceiling. Developing stylistic tendencies already affirmed in the *Doni Madonna* (Uffizi) and in the cartoon for the *Battle of Cascina,* the painter departs from the traditional 15th-century perspective vision. The diminution in the size of the figures towards the distance no longer corresponds to strict measure, but to a perspective arrived at by eye. The impression of depth is obtained through the play of masses in the imbalance created in the composition by the asymmetric mountains at the sides, with the void of the yawning stretch of water in the center. The figures unwind from group to group, the movement pausing and resuming, along a sort of giant reclining S. The space is thus dynamic, and makes a unity with the structure of the composition and the movement of the volumes. It is not a place assigned to the action or a theater for the drama, but the drama in itself as it rises and grows in pace with the development of the composition of the figures. From this comes the dominating impression of a limitless and disturbed space, the sense of tragedy that suffuses the whole and is everywhere evident in the details — in the mournful loosing of the figures from one another, in the twisting of the powerful bodies, in the intense tangle of limbs. Prevented by the scaffolding from checking the effect of his work at a distance, the artist painted many of the figures too small to be made out clearly and appreciated from the ground. But aside from this technical defect, which was immediately corrected in the succeeding scenes, the relationship between plastic and pictorial vision is perfectly in keeping with the expressive requirements. The nudes have the highest formal clarity; and in its dominant tonality between

MICHELANGELO
Drunkenness of Noah. The Flood
First and second of the biblical
scenes (counting from the entrance).
Frescoes. Executed probably from
August 1508 on.

terra cotta and a warm-marble patina punctuated with lighter accents, the color reinforces the sharpness of the forms.

MICHELANGELO. *Drunkenness of Noah.*

This is the last episode chronologically in the cycle, and probably the second to be painted; it represents the lapse into sin after the new covenant of Noah. The sin, it should be noted, according to the Bible did not lay in the drunkenness of the patriarch, but in the scorn of his son Ham, who presumed to deride his father's "shameful parts." Given Michelangelo's well-known preference for the nude and the classical aspect of the composition, and taking into account that the Bible does not stress the turpitude of Noah's nudity but the blasphemy of Ham, the unusual nudity of Noah's children is not surprising. Recalling Paolo Uccello's fresco in the Chiostro Verde, Michelangelo drew the hut in frontal perspective from close up, but by crowding the space forward with the large vat he could then dispose the scene according to the laws of ancient reliefs. It is typical that the perspective has no reference to the eye of the far-off spectator, and that the close-up view was chosen in order to give size to the foreground figures. The contrast between the animation of the sons' figures, with their springy flexible bodies, and the heavy figure of the old man, provides the dramatic quality of the scene, which is given a powerful moral tension by the grand simplicity of the composition.

84

MICHELANGELO
Detail of *The Flood.*

MICHELANGELO
Drunkenness of Noah
First scene (from entrance).
Fresco. Executed probably
from August 1508 on.

MICHELANGELO. *The Eritrean and Lybian Sibyls, the Prophets Jeremiah, Isaiah and Daniel.* *pp. 88/90*

In characterizing the Prophets and the Sibyls, the artist does not appear to have referred specifically to any prophecies attributed to them, nor to the subjects of the neighboring scenes: he intended rather to portray given moments in the life of prophecy. Thus the *Eritrean Sibyl,* moved by an unexpected impulse, comes to life in the act of looking for the answer to a mystery in her book. A superb image, inspired by the central nude in Signorelli's *Last Days of Moses,* it acquires dynamic unity from the down-curving right arm, reminiscent of the arm of *David.* In *Isaiah* the theme is the very arousal of prophetic inspiration, and this is stated not only illustratively by the book being closed as the Prophet turns at the call of a voice or a vision, but also is expressed in the formal structure. The spherical space enfolding the figure, and isolating it from the terrestrial space of the throne, is identified with a continuous and intense rotating motion emphasized by a vast spread of pink, counterpointed by the green accent of the mantle that provides an effect of isolation. The Soothsayers discussed up to now belong to the first phase of the work. The transition from the first to the second phase is marked also in the Prophets and the Sibyls by an increase in size, power

MICHELANGELO
The Eritrean and Libyan Sibyls
The Prophets Jeremiah and Isaiah
Frescoes.
The *Eritrean Sibyl* and *Isaiah* flank the *Sacrifice of Noah* (third scene from the entrance) and were executed probably in 1509. The *Jeremiah* and the *Libyan Sibyl* flank the *Separation of the Light from the Darkness* (last from the entrance) and were executed probably in 1512.

and profundity. An authentic prophetic furor is embodied in *Daniel* who pushes his legs out to the very edges of the throne, projects his torso forward and to the left, and has just removed his almost obsessed eyes from the enormous book that requires the added support of a putto-caryatid. The commanding figure of the *Libyan Sibyl* — which was studied, as a well-known drawing shows, from a nude model — is in the act of closing the book on the desk, and seems to be getting ready to descend from the throne and go into action. The elasticity of the contraposed movement is combined with a radiant sense of youthful, robust beauty, which is also conveyed by the luminous, predominantly warm hues of the robes, the vigorous turn of the bare shoulders and athletic arms. Contrasting with her, in type and in the moment of prophecy chosen, are the venerable old age and the closed construction of the *Jeremiah,* who is hunched over and absorbed in meditation. The blocked contraposition of the masses creates an exceptionally prominent plasticity, to which the lapidary intensity of the color and the restlessness of the two sad Virgins of Israel in the background contribute. Overhanging the altar wall is *Jonah,* symbol of the Resurrection, as he remained for three days in the belly of the whale, like Jesus in the tomb. But rather than Jonah's typological function, Michelangelo wants to stress his

89

MICHELANGELO
The Prophet Daniel
Detail, beside the scene of
the *Separation of the Dry Land
from the Waters.*
(seventh from entrance).
Fresco. Executed probably in 1512.

quarrel with the Lord, so as to repeat his constant thought that faith is a difficult and resistant conquest, as well as to conclude his series in a dramatically exalted atmosphere. An intense rotation, heightened by contrapuntal notes, unleashes here in a tempestuous finale the power accumulated in the entire sequence of the Soothsayers.

MICHELANGELO. *The Jesse Spandrel.*

It is part of the series of the Generations of Israel or the Ancestors of Christ, according to the first chapter of the Gospel of St. Matthew, along with the lunettes below. Here Jesse is the figure in shadow behind the woman, not named in Matthew, by whom Jesse generated King David, who is represented in the lunette below. Here at the margin of the grandiose fresco scheme, Michelangelo has given body to a modest and melancholy stock,

90

MICHELANGELO
The Jesse Spandrel
Spandrel corresponding to the scene
of the *Creation of the Planets.*
(next to the last from entrance).
Fresco. Executed probably in 1512.

untouched by the ray of divinity, which, in the long and only obscurely sensed expectation of the Redeemer, works out a dull and shrouded existence. To obtain this new expressive accent, Michelangelo has here, as often before, turned to the archaic austerity of Masaccio, broadening the range of formal inventions in a decidedly Manneristic direction. Art critics, falling into grave error, have sometimes mistaken the lesser formal tension of these figures for a sagging in the imaginative tension of the artist, but on the contrary, the compressed energy of these forms creates a new *terribilità* that is expressed in the grave silence of the images.

MICHELANGELO
The Punishment of Haman
Pendentive to right of altar wall.
Fresco. Executed probably in 1512.

MICHELANGELO. *The Punishment of Haman — The Brazen Serpent*

pp. 92/95

Four "miraculous salvations of Israel" occupy the pendentives connecting the vault and the walls. On the two to the sides of the entrance are represented the slaying of Holofernes by Judith and that of Goliath by David; the two on the altar side of the chapel represent the subjects named above. *The Punishment of Haman* portrays, as recounted in the Book of Esther, the execution of the Vizier Haman. Haman hated Mordecai because he refused to bow, as Haman had required all the courtiers to do; to revenge this affront Haman had obtained from the cruel Persian King Ahasuerus a free hand over the Jews, and had ordered their massacre, reserving for Mordecai death by hanging from a gallows erected for that purpose in the house of Haman himself. By the miraculous effect of lamentations and fasts that Mordecai ordered the Jewish people to perform, Queen Esther, his cousin, who had been in disgrace for some time, was received by her royal master, could invite the king to banquet with Mordecai, convince him of the perfidy of the Vizier and obtain the revocation of the decreed massacre and the punishment of Haman. Meanwhile, Ahasuerus, reading one sleepless night the book of chronicles, learns that it was Mordecai who some time back had discovered and exposed a plot against him, and orders that great honor be done to him. The complicated story is synthesized by the painter as follows: on the left Esther, at table with Ahasuerus, denounces Haman; in the center the execution of the Vizier; on the right Ahasuerus listens to the

reading of the chronicles and sends for Mordecai. *The Brazen Serpent* illustrates the story told in Numbers, XXI. The Jewish people, discouraged on their journey, had taken to murmuring against Moses and blaspheming God. For this, Jehovah sent swarms of poisonous serpents against his people, who were slaughtered. Moved to pity, Moses erected a pole and upon it put a serpent of brass, which had the virtue of saving from death those who had been bitten by the snakes, if they looked at it. The two scenes, situated as has been said above the altar wall, probably prefigure in some way the Crucifixion of Christ (in both the tree trunk and the pole the allusion to the Cross is obvious); whereas together with the other two "salvations" they more generally prefigure the Redemption. Both compositions share in the dramatic furor that animates the adjoining figure of the Prophet Jonah, constituting together a sort of triptych in which the accumulated tensions in the representation of the entire vault are discharged with extraordinary intensity. In the one as well as the other, critics have recognized an echo, at a distance, of the enormous impression made on the artists, and in particular on Michelangelo, by the discovery, in 1506, of the Hellenistic group of the *Laocoön*. Almost all the groups on the right in *The Brazen Serpent* are like a series of brilliant variations on the theme of the *Laocoön,* while the crucified Haman is evidently inspired by the principal figure in the ancient statuary group. Here it should be observed how Michelangelo — with a skill dissimulated by the impetus of the invention and fantasy — has not only overcome but positively exploited the difficulties inherent in the fact that the figure falls on either side of the conjunction of the two curved surfaces of the pendentive. As early as 1760, Bottari had observed: "It is painted in the corner of the chapel, and is half on one surface and half on another, and by dint of perspective seems all to be on the same plane." The dynamic tension in the two compositions is such as to throw the space into confusion and to shatter every limit of classical propriety. And this is true for the *Punishment of Haman* despite the fact that the compositional framework preserved the memory of Giotto's highly balanced and calibrated composition of the *Birth of John the Baptist* in the Peruzzi Chapel. And it is also possible that Michelangelo, in assimilating the execution of Haman to a crucifixion, had remembered, ardent reader of Dante as he was, the vision referring to the punishment of Ire in the XVII canto of the *Purgatory:* "Next shower'd into my fantasy a shape/ As of one crucified, whose visage spake/ Fell rancor, malice deep, wherein he died." The figure of Haman in torment appears as proudly rebellious. From an abstractly formal point of view, these two scenes go beyond the poetic creativity of the Renaissance and are part of Mannerism; in fact they offered schooling to the Mannerists of successive decades. In their substance, however, they cannot be called Mannerist, because the violence of the expression was not reflected or indirect, but gushed directly from the tormented mind of Michelangelo.

MICHELANGELO
The Brazen Serpent
Pendentive to left of altar wall.
94 Fresco. Executed probably in 1512.

MICHELANGELO. *The Last Judgment.*

On the commission received in the autumn of 1533 from Clement VII and confirmed by his successor, Paul III, Michelangelo, after three years of meditation and preliminary drawings, carried out from 1536 to 1541 the fresco of the *Last Judgment* on the altar wall of the Sistine Chapel. The distance between the artist's two major works in painting would appear to be unbridgeable if measured from the portrayals of the Creation — mournfully dramatic but also animated by a joyous vitality — to the lowering and desperate atmosphere of the *Last Judgment*. If, however, one starts from the existential melancholy of the Generations of Israel, and follows in the *Slaves* and *Prisoners* for the tomb of Pope Julius and in the Medici tombs the gradual recovery of vital tension against a constant background of closed and mournful meditation, the *Last Judgment* will appear as the culminating manifestation in a long process of development in the spirit of Michelangelo. He had been sorely tried in those decades by misfortunes in Florence and in his family; and disheartened as to the validity of human endeavor, was ever more inclined to seek refuge in an unattainable mystic identification with God. Giving up any frame for the composition — by requiring an illusionary reading from the spectator, this would have led to the vision of a limited even though vast space — the painter floods the entire immense wall with an open and unlimited space, abolishing any measurable relationship with the figures and evoking the image of an abysmal void, in which swim, desperately alone in the midst of a crowd, the bodies of the risen, isolated within separate plastic organisms. The torrents and the whirling stream of the figures in the celestial court rushing toward Christ, the fall of the damned to the right and the ascent of the blessed to the left — all happens against the background of a limitless and perturbed space, evoked by the audacious and complex foreshortening of the figures. A truly cosmic force is unleashed by the measured and terrible gesture of the *Judge,* impressing upon the universe an irresistible rotatory movement which goes on not with the tranquil regularity of a phenomenon of gravity but with the uncontrolled fury of a universal catastrophe. This unleashing of forces acquires an overwhelming power by submitting to the control of art, in a compositional fabric that is very solid and worked on the principle of counterpoint. A dialectic between outbursts of unchecked movement and motives of stops and balances dominates the separate figures as well as the relationships between the parts of the composition. The elliptical motion of the *Saints* and *Patriarchs* around the *Judge* is broadened in the external ellipse formed above by the most distant figures running up, and below by the righteous ascending and the sinners falling. The hinge is the group of the *Trumpeting Angels* at the lower center, from which two descending obliques depart — marked by the lines of the trumpets — thus establishing the link between the lower level containing the *Resurrection of the Dead, Charon's Boat, Minos* and the *Mouths of Hell.* But groups of the risen on the left and the damned on the right provide transition to the vertical action of the righteous and the sinners in the zone above, creating an interlace and interaction of force and directions. The *Angels* in the lunettes are part of this, too, as the Cross and the column they are carrying offer two diagonal directions, which are immediately interrupted by the vortex of figures below but echoed farther down by the two already cited obliques.

MICHELANGELO
The Last Judgment
1536–1541
Fresco; height 44′, 11 1/4″;
width about 43′, 4″.

MICHELANGELO.   *Christ as Judge and the Virgin.*

In the anti-classical context of the *Last Judgment,* inspiration from the antique bursts forth in the *Christ,* and this is made more evident in the contrast with the serpentine module — already Mannerist in taste — of the figure of the *Virgin.* A dynamic image, it is perfectly balanced in a position between that of a standing and a seated figure, caught in the moment of getting up while raising its right hand in the gesture of condemnation and calling the righteous with its left. The circle described by the opposite motion of the arms holds it in balance and gives it majesty, and the balance is repeated, discreetly, by the unaccented counterposition of the arms and legs. Collected in this image and translated into contained tension, is all the terrible force that is dispersed in the universe of hundreds of figures. Thus the action of *Christ the Judge* as an immobile motor is restated figuratively.

MICHELANGELO
Christ as Judge, and the Virgin
Detail of *The Last Judgment.*

99

MICHELANGELO. *The Righteous — The Sinners — The Risen Dead*

pp. 100/102

The figures, although sometimes entwined with one another, clearly allude to the isolation of the plastic block: each of them is, like a statue, perfectly defined in its contours. Occasionally, as in the famous figure of a damned soul seated on a bank of clouds (p. 101), the sense of the block is so strong as to evoke images of stone in the mind. But even in the more impetuous figures, the contrapositions and the spiraling movements obey the same laws as the unfinished *Prisoners,* straining with the effort to free themselves from the material. Each of these figures may thus appear to be closed within the paradigm of the solution of a problem in form, but they should be seen in their reciprocal relationships, linked together by the requirements of expression and drama, and immersed in space by means of the foreshortenings and the complex fabric of oblique movements of the whole.

MICHELANGELO
The Risen Dead
Detail of *The Last Judgment.*

MICHELANGELO
Charon's Boat
Detail of *The Last Judgment.*

MICHELANGELO. *Charon's Boat.*

"Charon in demonic form, with eyes of glowing coal, collects them all/ Beckoning, and each that lingers, with his oar strikes." It would be pedantic to deny, though it has been attempted, the inspiration from Dante in this group, with the pretext that here Charon "with his oar strikes" the souls disembarking and not, as in Dante, during their embarkation. This is poetic license, easily explained by the artist's intention to utilize Charon's brandished oar as a link with the "crescendo" accompanying the descent to hell of the damned souls, who farther down are being dragged to the lowest depths by devils. That Michelangelo was an ardent reader of Dante, indeed an esteemed Dantean, is attested if only by Gianotti's *Dialogues,* and it is obvious that beyond any precise references, throughout the fresco there is the suggestion of a Dantesque spirit. The inexorable force of portrayal, the unadorned simplicity of style, the absence of moralistic scruples (the "great stew of nudes" censured by detractors!) in the high morality of the conception — all these have the savor of Dante. In contrast with the left-hand area, where the awakening of the dead follows a slow and sluggish rhythm, here the action becomes hurried, in the crowded and compact scene.

MICHELANGELO
Resurrection of the Flesh
Detail of *The Last Judgment.*

MICHELANGELO
Head of a Damned Soul in the Cave of Hell
Detail of *The Last Judgment.*

MICHELANGELO. *Detail of the Resurrection of the Flesh — Head of a Damned Soul in the Cave of Hell.*

The slow and torpid motions of the dead awakened by the trumpets of the Last Judgment, who arise and whose skeletons are being clothed again in flesh, prepare the increasingly quick and light movements of the figures — still on the left — immediately above the righteous, that are being almost sucked up by the call of the Judge. It is in this area of the immense composition that the figures are fewer, and the thinning out of the bodies exposes more sky, opening towards the bottom a desperately profound space that is a prelude to the manner of composing the two frescoes in the Pauline Chapel. The group of the risen skeleton and the man already clad in flesh but still reclining, makes up a prominent outlying composition on the earthly horizon, but behind it the body that has taken flight penetrates obliquely into the depths of the sky, arousing a sense of infinite space. The head of the damned soul in the cave, glowing like a spectre of death in the dark, is among the master's most impressive images.

105

MICHELANGELO. *Crucifixion of St. Peter — Fresco in the Pauline Chapel.*
A year after the completion of the *Last Judgment,* in November 1542, Michelangelo began to fresco the Pauline Chapel. This is, however, the second fresco, in order of execution, which took place from the spring of 1546 until early in 1550. The space is deep and limitless but establishes no formal relationship with the spectator, because of the absence of a fixed point of view; rather it includes the spectator through the cutting of the groups of figures in the foreground by the bottom of the scene. Around the cross that penetrates into the background obliquely and provides the main movement in the composition, revolve the figures of soldiers and mourners. In addition to the rotary motion on the level plane there is the suggestion of a ver-

MICHELANGELO
Crucifixion of St. Peter
Fresco: 20′, 6″ × 21′, 8″.
Pauline Chapel.

tical rotation in the cross being raised by the executioners, which in turn evokes a spherical and cosmic vision of space. By means of the iconographical innovation of showing the cross before its erection, the artist was able to make the head and bold eyes of Peter the fulcrum of the composition, and dynamically portray the action of the scene without relinquishing the fundamental point of the spiritual triumph of the martyr. The figures are not the traditional onlookers; they seem to be arriving from far away and to be going on somewhere, appalled and bewildered, disarmed in the face of crime. This is expressed in the blocking out of the masses in compact sculptural formations, almost metaphysical in aspect, and in the corresponding stiffening of the faces in dehumanized dismay.

MICHELANGELO
Group of Onlookers
Detail of the *Crucifixion of St. Peter.*

107

MICHELANGELO. *The Conversion of St. Paul — Pauline Chapel.*

It was painted from 1542 to 1546. Not only God the Father, upside down in the sky, but also the extreme agitation and the unbridled movement recall the *Last Judgment*. The instantaneous culmination of the miracle finds expression in the centrifugal composition of the lower zone, to which is counterpointed the centripetal movement of the celestial scene. The absence of exact perspective points of reference and the cutting of the two soldiers by the lower edge of the scene, bring the spectator into immediate contact with the emotion aroused by the miracle. The scene is thus not conceived as a historical event but as a mystic experience for the onlooker.

MICHELANGELO
The Conversion of St. Paul
1542–1546
Fresco: 20′, 6″ × 21′, 8″.
Pauline Chapel.

RAPHAEL'S STANZE

DISPUTATION OF THE SACRAMENT.   *pp. 110/113*

Constructed by Nicholas I, the Stanze had already been partially decorated by Piero della Francesca, Andrea del Castagno and Benedetto Bonfigli, when Pope Julius II had the fresco decoration resumed — in 1508 — by a group of artists recommended by Bramante, among whom were Perugino, Sodoma, Bramantino, Baldassare Peruzzi, Lorenzo Lotto, Giovanni Ruysch and Michele del Becca. The initiative was due to the fact that the new Pope, as Paolo Giovio reports: ". . . did not want to see at every moment . . . the figure of his predecessor, Alexander, his enemy, and called him *marrano,* Jew and circumcised." He could not have been very satisfied with the first list, but accepted Bramante's new suggestion to call in Raphael, who had become the most prominent personality in Florentine painting.

The *Disputation of the Sacrament* (so called through a false 17th-century interpretation of a passage in Vasari) was the first scene to be frescoed by the Urbino master. The scene is set out of doors, around an altar on which is a monstrance with the Host, which is the single perspective center of the entire complex and harmonious composition, from the geometric foreground of the steps to the landscape in the rear and the vault of heaven. Taking their points of departure from the Host, as if in intermittent waves, are the aureole of the Holy Ghost and the great nimbus of Christ in Glory,

RAPHAEL
Urbino 1483 — Rome 1520
Disputation of the Sacrament
Stanza della Segnatura
Detail.
Fresco in lunette: 25′ 3 1/4″.

RAPHAEL
Disputation of the Sacrament
Detail.

which seems to expand, by reflection, in the arched wall, a simulated architectural opening, an ideal arch of triumph. In plan, a formally geometric marble pavement, suggesting nostalgia for basilican space, is connected as by allegory with the images of buildings in construction scattered in the landscape, and the "architecture" of the figures in air. Seated on a balcony of zephyrs, as if portrayed in the shell of an imaginary apse, they are part of an ensemble suspended from above, that in turn recalls a half-lowered theater curtain. In this painting there is evidently an echo of the great excitement over the new St. Peter's, which was being built.

The *Disputation* is painted in a style that is still clearly of Florentine extraction, with reminiscences of Leonardo, Fra Bartolomeo, Andrea del Sarto and even more remote recollections going back to the artist's studies with Perugino. But the work has a monumentality not seen before, the courtly spirit of a history painter, and above all a surprising novelty in imagery.

RAPHAEL
Disputation of the Sacrament
Detail.
Portrait of Dante.

RAPHAEL
Disputation of the Sacrament
Detail.

THE SCHOOL OF ATHENS.

pp. 114/117

In the fresco of *The School of Athens* Raphael shows an ever-increasing interest in Michelangelo's style and methods, culminating in the homage of painting the master's portrait in the guise of Heraclitus, which he included in the fresco probably after seeing part of the Sistine ceiling in 1510. The figure does not appear in the preparatory cartoon now in the Pinacoteca Ambrosiana, Milan. Nor does the architecture of the background, whose entirely new character, that is its wholly un-Utopian aspect, gives credence to the hypothesis that it is a view of St. Peter's following Bramante's project, as its resemblance to the section by Peruzzi in the Uffizi confirms. It cannot be excluded that the pope wished to see a view of the edifice as it would be on completion, but utilized here in the context of his political and cultural program, which is in fact the theme of this hall.

Apart from this, the independence of Raphael's style with respect to Michelangelo's was already pointed out by Vasari, when he stated that Raphael: "considered that painting does not consist merely in making nudes. Its field is broader and among perfect painters are those who can express, well and

RAPHAEL
The School of Athens
Detail.

easily, all the inventions in a story and its many variations with good judgment. In the composition of the scenes one who knows how not to confuse with too much and also not to make them too poor with too little, may be called a valiant and judicious master. . . . He considered, too, how important . . . it is to make portraits that appear to be alive. In truth, in him we have art, color and invention . . . brought to that end and perfection for which one could scarcely have hoped, nor should anyone think ever to surpass him." It is interesting at this point to observe how the philosophers and sages of antiquity, in the elect assembly, are represented by eminent contemporary personalities, according to a sort of Platonic reincarnation; and among them artists are portrayed (including the self-portrait of Raphael), to indicate the ideological nature of painting. The success of this work was enormous. As Vasari mentions, Julius II wanted ". . . to tear down all the scenes of the other masters, old and modern, so that Raphael alone would have the glory of all the labors that had gone into those works up until that time." And certainly what astonished the pontiff and the scholars of the court (among them Bembo, Bibbiena, Castiglione and Inghirami) could not have been only the excellence of the painting, but the discovery of new possibilities of life, the effective illustration of the ideal Hellenism which was sought after, but which no one as yet had succeeded in visualizing in so stimulating and disturbing a form. It is obvious that the pope's enjoyment of the work did not depend only on its expressive quality, but above all on the subject matter and the concepts which certainly no one else had achieved with such keen, full-bodied and convincing lyricism.

117

PARNASSUS.

Parnassus is an archeological theme in literature, from Homer to Virgil, from Dante to Petrarch and the Petrarchists of the 16th century, yet Raphael had the ability to bring it up to date in the form of the humanistic "repose" especially dear to the authors of the dialogues on poetics as an ideal milieu. Mythological divinities, ancient seers and modern poets may thus find themselves all together, in good company. As in a dream, the figures in the party with their vital, almost magnetic presence, spangle the serene landscape. Opposite *Parnassus,* the *Theological Virtues* are painted above the window overlooking the Belvedere. Thus the decoration of the Stanza della Segnatura (so designated after the ecclesiastical tribunal of the same name, which according to tradition subsequently sat here, although the hall was originally intended for the pontifical library) followed a specific cultural program, in as much as it illustrated the supreme truths, *Revealed Truth* and *Natural Truth, Beauty* and *Justice,* to which corresponded on the ceiling the respective allegories of *Theology, Philosophy, Poetry* and *Justice,* as in a sort of *speculum doctrinale* — Mirror of Doctrine. As the major and minor representations are linked ideologically, so Raphael shows that he conceived them in a single formal plan, in as much as the lunette scenes are arranged around the real cubic space of the hall like satellite exedras in a centralized architectural system, which was one of the major subjects of inquiry among the architects of the period.

RAPHAEL
Parnassus
Stanza della Segnatura
Fresco in lunette: 21' 12" at base.

RAPHAEL
Parnassus
Detail of the Muses.

RAPHAEL
Parnassus
Detail with heads of
Corinna, Petrarch and Anacreon.

RAPHAEL
Urbino 1482 — Rome 1520
GIULIO ROMANO
Rome 1492 — Mantua 1546
*Expulsion of Heliodorus from
the Temple*
Stanza di Eliodoro
Fresco in lunette: 24′ 7″ at base.

GIULIO ROMANO
Expulsion of Heliodorus
Detail.

RAPHAEL AND ASSISTANTS
Meeting of Attila and St. Leo
Stanza di Eliodoro
Fresco in lunette: 24′ 7″ at base.

EXPULSION OF HELIODORUS FROM THE TEMPLE.

The *Expulsion of Heliodorus from the Temple* gives the name of Heliodorus to this Stanza, painted between 1511 and 1514, in which are represented other closely related themes (*Miraculous Mass of Bolsena, Deliverance of St. Peter, Meeting of Attila and St. Leo*) that appear to have their connection in another aspect of the pope's program — this time political and religious — and allude in these early years of Reformation unrest to an intransigent attitude in defense of the Roman papacy.

The part most surely by the hand of Raphael seems to be the group on the left, which is connected with the adjoining *Miraculous Mass of Bolsena* by its brilliant color. Below it is written the date of 1514, year of the succession of the new pontiff, Leo X (following the death of Julius II in 1513), who had continued the work of decoration, but obviously not without having a say in its conception. In this painting he seems to be present at the biblical event as an outsider, a spectator; in reality the figure may be a later addition, as it masks part of the superb group behind, which was certainly conceived by Raphael but probably executed by others. Traces of alterations, indeed of a real reworking, are also found in the group on the right, behind the actual version which is attributed to Giulio Romano, and it does reflect his statuesque late Roman classicism (note the recollection of the *Laocoön* and of the Trajanic relief on the Arch of Constantine).

121

MEETING OF ATTILA AND ST. LEO.   *p. 120*

In this fresco, the conception is the master's as are a few passages in the
painting (on the left, for example), but much of the work is by assistants,
who are generally held to be Giulio Penni and Giulio Romano. Along with
lesser artists, they had responsibility for the execution of the successive
Stanze, beginning with the Stanza dell'Incendio Borgo. Raphael had, in fact,
taken on at this period a truly enormous number of professional assign-
ments, but the phenomenon is not to be explained only pragmatically, by
this burden; another reason is the lesser interest at the time in work by an
artist's own hand than in the paternity of the idea behind the work. In this
way Raphael used his assistants in the fashion of an architect on a building
project, that is simply superintending a crew of skilled artisans in the execution of his ideas.

RAPHAEL
Deliverance of St. Peter
Stanza di Eliodoro
Detail.

DELIVERANCE OF ST. PETER.

A vision as stylistically new and bold as the St. Peter scenes must have been
stimulated by an encounter with Venetian painting, especially with the luminous qualities of Sebastiano del Piombo, who had come to Rome in 1511.
Commenting on the painting, Vasari gives the following superb description: ". . . the horror of the prison, on seeing the old man bound with
iron chains between the two men in armor; the deep sleep of the guards;
and the shining splendor of the angel in the dark shadows of the night, lu-
minously brings out all the details of the prison and makes the armor of the
guards glitter so intensely that the sheen seems more burnished than if it
were real. . . . Nor is there less art and intellect in the scene where, the
chains having been loosed, he comes out of the prison, accompanied by the
angel, and has the look on his face of it all being a dream, rather than reality. How great the terror and fright of those other armed guards outside the
prison, when they hear the noise of the iron door, as a sentry with a torch
wakes them, making a whisp of light which is echoed in every weapon, and
what the torch does not touch, the light of the moon reaches. Raphael having painted this invention above the window, and the wall thus being dark,
when you look at the picture it lights your face. And the painted light with
different night effects competes so well with the living light that you seem
to see the smoke of the torch, the splendor of the angel and the dark shadow
of the night, all so natural and real that you would never say they were
painted, so exactly has such a difficult fancy been expressed. In the armor,
the shadows, the reflections and the luminosity of the warmth of the lights
are so dazzlingly executed, that truly it may be said that he was the master
of all others. And for a thing which counterfeited night more closely than
has even been done in painting, this is the most divine, and held by all to
be the most exceptional."

122

GIULIO ROMANO AND RAPHAEL
Fire in the Borgo
Stanza dell 'Incendio Borgo
Fresco in lunette: 21' 12" at base.

It should be noted that this highly interesting representation is not so much a fanciful novelty as a renewal of a vein of luministic painting that goes from Giotto in the Bardi *Stigmata* to Taddeo and Agnolo Gaddi, and from the latter to Piero della Francesca, who repeats the nocturnal scene in his *Dream of Constantine*. With Raphael it returns as a form of realism obeying the needs of the nocturnal episode and connected with the prison theme — ancestor of a form of expression that from Caravaggio to Piranese, with his visionary spectacles of Roman prisons, will become a pictorial genre. It should also be noted how Raphael introduced the type of continuous narration, to express more vividly the effects, as in dreams and mystic visions, of doubling the image of a person; the duality is then reabsorbed by the enveloping penumbra. This is one of the great pages in Western art.

FIRE IN THE BORGO.
It is the last work in the Vatican Stanze that has the savor of Raphael, and gives its name to the room; it was executed between 1514 and 1517. For this room, scenes showing popes of the name of Leo were planned, in honor of Leo X. The present episode refers to a miracle attributed to Leo IV, who by appearing and giving his benediction was said to have extinguished a dangerous fire that had broken out in the populous Borgo quarter. In the background the pope appears in the loggia of a Raphaelesque palace and beyond is discernible the façade of the Constantinian Basilica of St. Peter.

GIULIO ROMANO AND RAPHAEL
Fire in the Borgo
Detail of the Aeneas group.

125

The project seems unquestionably to be Raphael's and has a distinct stage-set and antiquarian flavor, probably relating to his renewed archeological interests and to the new Latinizing culture of Leo X. Thus the chronicle of the miracle is identified with the myth of the burning of Troy, and on the left appears the celebrated Virgilian group of Aeneas, fleeing with his family. The execution of the foreground figures is attributed to Giulio Romano, the rest to Giulio Penni. It is interesting to note that in the formative process of Picasso's *Guernica,* the memory of the episode of the child handed over the wall crops up again.

RAPHAEL
Miraculous Mass of Bolsena
Stanza di Eliodoro
Detail of Chair Bearers
Fresco.

MIRACULOUS MASS OF BOLSENA.

In the *Miraculous Mass of Bolsena,* one of the most sublime frescoes of the entire cycle, the neo-Venetian color experiments begun around 1511–12 and here related in particular to Titian and Lotto, come to maturity.

Like the other scenes in the Stanza di Eliodoro, this one belongs to the series of miracles serving as apologia for orthodoxy, which was undergoing considerable shock. If the episodes of the *Expulsion of Heliodorus from the Temple* and the *Meeting of Attila and St. Leo* had a flavor of almost nationalistic defiance, in the sense of "out with the barbarians," the present scene was dedicated to the defense of the fundamental mystery of the Catholic Church: the Eucharist. It represents a miracle that took place in 1263, when a Bohemian priest, tormented by doubts on the truth of transubstantiation, while journeying from Prague to Rome celebrated mass at Bolsena. He then saw blood drip from the consecrated Host and bathe the corporal. The miracle also had important consequences for art: St. Thomas Aquinas composed two hymns (*Sing, my tongue the Savior's glory* and *Sion lift thy voice and sing*) for the mass of the feast of Corpus Domini, instituted ad hoc by Urban IV in 1264; in its honor the Cathedral of Orvieto was built, its reliquary fashioned by Ugolino di Vieri, and the present fresco painted.

The composition, as in the case of the *Parnassus* and the *Deliverance of St. Peter,* was organically adapted to the limited space of the wall, which is cut by a window. The scene is thus disposed to include two approaches, at the sides, leading to the center of interest above — the altar with its background of a curving parapet. The details of the groups at the side are splendid: the one on the left for its quietly stirring animation; that on the right for the beauty of the portraits of the cardinals and the abstract, unmoved dignity of the chair-bearers.

THE FALL. THE JUDGMENT OF SOLOMON. *pp. 128–129*

The two paintings on the ceiling of the Stanza della Segnatura alternate with two other emblematic episodes (*Astronomy, Apollo and Marsyas*) in the vault sections and with those bearing the tondi of *Philosophy, Theology,*

etc., all part of the complicated doctrinal program of the decoration. The figures in these scenes are cut out against simulated gold mosaic backgrounds and are of a clearly didactic kind but not less beautiful for this. Indeed they played a highly important part as forerunners of numerous illustrated editions of the Bible.

POETRY. PHILOSOPHY.   *pp. 128/130*

The allegory of *Poetry* is an inspired figure (the inscription reads: *numine afflatur* — Virgil, Aeneid, VI, 50 — following the conception of the Platonic Phedra) with burning eyes and wings to indicate flights of the imagination. The allegory of *Philosophy* (*causarum cognitio* — "cognition of causes") is a pensive figure holding two volumes to indicate the branches of natural and moral philosophy, and is seated on a Neo-Classical throne supported by two figures of the Diana of Ephesus, derived from the antique (like many other details taken from ancient marbles in these paintings, from the *Parnassus* to the *Meeting of Attila and St. Leo,* as Vasari originally pointed out). The colors and embroidery of the figure's robes symbolize the four elements. The division of the vault, and its decoration with grotesques, had already been carried out, apparently by Bramantino — by Sodoma some believe — when Raphael began his work.

RAPHAEL
Poetry. Ceiling fresco in
Stanza della Segnatura.

RAPHAEL
The Fall. Detail.
Stanza della Segnatura

RAPHAEL
The Judgment of Solomon
Stanza della Segnatura.

On page 130:
RAPHAEL
Philosophy. Ceiling fresco in
Stanza della Segnatura.

PINACOTECA
CHAPEL OF NICHOLAS V
BORGIA APARTMENTS

JOHANNES AND NICOLAUS. *The Last Judgment.*

This tondo, unusual in its rectangular appendix at the base, is one of the most ancient Western representations — in large format — of the *Last Judgment,* and contains motives of great interest concerning iconographic innovation and the choice of illustrative inscriptions, both as to text and type of letters. In five superposed bands, reading from the top down, the following subjects are represented: the apparition of *Christ in Glory;* the *Divine Tribunal; Madonna with the Resurrected* and scenes of three works of charity — *Giving Drink to the Thirsty, Visiting Prisoners, Clothing the Naked;* the *Resurrection of the Dead;* and, in the predella below, *Paradise* to the left and *Hell* on the right. The two artists' mastery of style is seen in the sureness with which the scenes are linked, utilizing devices that presuppose a broad acquaintanceship with contemporary wall decoration, as well as with ancient examples of vase painting. They make fluid transitions from composed and symmetrically disposed images to those that are more intensely animated, as in the *Resurrection,* where animals, fish and birds disgorge bit by bit the parts of human beings they have devoured, or in the gloomy smoldering cave of *Hell,* crammed with damned souls feeling the fangs and being drawn into the coils of a long serpent. A Latin inscription includes the signature of the two authors: "At the sound of the trumpet they rise from the dust of the earth. Nicolaus and Johannes, painters."

JOHANNES AND NICOLAUS
Rome, 11th–12th century
(dating controversial).
Last Judgment (11th century?).
Canvas on panel: 9′ 6″ × 7′ 11″.
Provenance: S. Maria in
Campo Marzio, Rome.

JOHANNES AND NICOLAUS
Detail of *Last Judgment*
The Resurrection of the Dead.

+REGNVMPERCIPITE·BENEDICTIQVIQ·VENITE· VOBISPARATVM·PERSECLAC VNCTADONATVM·

OFFERET·VT·PAVLVS·FVERITO DQ·VISQ·LVCRATVS·QD·MARTYR·STEPHANVS·CLAMAT GREX·ISTEPVSILLV·MEQ·A·PAVISTI·POTV·PSEPEDEDISTE·VEL·SIMVL·IN DVTO·REPARASTI·CORPEREN·VO

OMEGENVS VOLVCR V V ELREP TILISATO FERAR V REDIVNT HVMANA·PISCES·QVOQ·MENBRA·VORATA
ANCOR ET TVBAE SVRGVNT DETVLVEL ET·PITE·NICOLAVSIOHS·PIC

TIS·IS·T ES PARADISC RES HOS B LISTRA

GIOTTO. *The Stefaneschi Polyptych.*   *pp. 134/136*

The monumental triptych that Cardinal Stefaneschi commissioned Giotto to paint in 1298 was intended for the spacious Constantinian Basilica of St. Peter. Painted on both sides, on one it shows *Christ Enthroned with Angels and Stefaneschi in Adoration* in the center and to the right and to the left, the *Martyrdoms of St. Peter and St. Paul;* on the other side, *St. Peter in Benediction with Angels, Saints and Donor* and to the right and to the left, *St. Andrew and St. John the Evangelist, St. James and St. Paul.* Numerous figures of saints, angels and prophets are included in the pilasters, medallions, pinnacles and predella. It is not surprising that Giotto, as the critics have ascertained, loaded at this moment of his maturity with commissions, entrusted the execution of the grandiose project to several of his most gifted students (Bernardo Daddi has been mentioned as one of them). He himself, however, determined and drew up the composition, and certainly followed the various phases of the execution. Giotto's most extensive firsthand participation is seen in the central panel of Christ, whose majestic pyramidal structure echoes the profile of the pinnacle. The dimensionality of the picture, already articulated by the outward-projecting arms and powerful knees of the central figure, is also achieved through the spacing of the minor figures; the foreshortening of the steps and of the carpet with its flattened squares; and above all by the sharp convergence of the sides of the throne, that are cut off at the top to suggest the separation between the plane closest to the spectator, which is that of the frame, and the more distant planes that progressively merge into undefined golden space.

In some of the lateral sections appear isolated instances of the students' specific inclinations: a contour emphasized more insistently at the curves and angles; the development of the color in a lighter value, with sharp clear accents and minute luminous flushes in the faces, whose dramatically fixed expression is thus emphasized. Nevertheless, the plan and structure are Giotto's: in the *Martyrdom of St. Paul* (p. 136) note the affinity in structure between the two compact groups of figures connected at the center by the body of the saint lying prone, and the two heights behind them — sketched in broad planes — diverging upward from the saddle of the hill and prolonged by the cylindrical forms of the crumbling tower on the right, by the pious woman catching the saint's mantle on the left. Typical of the master is the choice of moment in illustrating the martyrdom of St. Paul. It is not the capture or the slaying, but the moment immediately afterward, when his head has already rolled on the ground, his disciples are bowed in silence and the soldiers are getting ready to go back, impassive like the cutthroat in the foreground shown in the act of sheathing his sword.

VITALE DA BOLOGNA. *Madonna and Child.*   *p. 137*

The recovery of the personality of Vitale and the recognition of the exceptional part he played around the middle of the 14th century, are recent discoveries in art scholarship. Educated in a milieu that had the benefit of the presence and wide-ranging interests of the University of Bologna, he retained his Romanesque and Giottesque heritage. At the same time he was familiar with other currents of taste and adopted Gothic elements — French and Bohemian — though not forgetting that the substratum of this style, soon to become international in character, was Sienese. In this *Madonna,*

GIOTTO AND ASSISTANTS
Colle di Vespignano 1266 — Florence 1337
Detail of the Stefaneschi Polyptych: *Christ Enthroned with Angels and Cardinal Jacopo Stefaneschi*
(ca. 1330–1335)
Panel: 7' 2" × 8'. Commissioned for the Great Altar of St. Peter's by Cardinal Stefaneschi, who paid 400 gold florins for it.

which belongs to the artist's early maturity, Vitale appears to bridle his lively powers of invention to turn to meditate more deeply on the works of Simone Martini. Moreover the image has more body, a compactness that stands out in the smooth ovals of the faces, in the thick edges of the robes, in the long fingers of the Virgin that rise to close the curvilinear cadences.

GIOVANNI DI PAOLO. *Nativity.*   *p. 138*
Giovanni di Paolo was the solitary creator of lunar landscapes, exquisite narrator of miraculous happenings where not only the event, but also the place, the time, the persons and the things are described in irrational terms. He carried the refined Sienese tradition to its limit, sustained on the course of his free expression by the examples of Gentile da Fabriano and Lorenzo

Monaco. In this *Nativity,* Giovanni does not set the scene on a ground plane, but allows each element to float in penumbra. Gigantic hedges of roses smother the fragile shed, the thin walls and the minute grotto, pushing the protagonists towards the foreground and sending the shepherds listening to the good tidings back towards the pale blue hills. There is no communication among the various figures, and the light, heightening the colors against a dark ground, accentuates their isolation.

NICCOLÒ ALUNNO. *Crucifixion.*

The intense expressionism that characterizes the school of Foligno, and in some aspects the arts of Umbria and the Marches, found vibrant support in the 15th century in the activity of the Veneto painter, Crivelli. Besides, this was an attitude that was already present in the area, as testified by the works of Niccolò Alunno, popularizer of a culture that attempted to reconcile the

GIOVANNI DI PAOLO
Siena 1395/1400–1482
Nativity (ca. 1436–1440)
Predella panel. 16″ × 13″.
Other panels of the same predella are in the Berlin and Cleveland museums, and in the Kress and Blumenthal Collections (Metropolitan Museum New York).

NICCOLÒ ALUNNO
(NICCOLÒ DI LIBERATORE)
Foligno ca. 1430–1502
Crucifixion (ca. 1490)
Detail of a *Triptych*.
Panel: 10′ 10″ × 15′ 9″. In the lateral panels
are represented the figures of St. John the
Baptist, St. Porphyrius, St. Peter and St. Ve-
nantius. Executed for the church of S. Ve-
nanzio at Camerino.

conflicting aims of the Florentine school (disseminated in Umbria by
Benozzo Gozzoli) and those of the Vivarini school, which found a persist-
ing vitality in the late Gothic style. This may help to clarify why in the triptych under discussion — represented here by the most violent and aggres-
sive part of the central panel of the *Crucifixion* — is intermingled with contrasting elements: a Renaissance conception of space seen specifically in the
arrangement of the figures, especially in the foreshortening of the heads,
and in the broad declivities of the hilly landscape. These are an insistent,
agitated elaboration of the paint itself, resplendent with metallic glints, and
a violent, truly medieval emphasis on the drama, which flows forth in episodes revealing a fervent and at the same time cruel devotion — such as the
angels, solidly perched on the clouds, who hold up precious vessels to collect the blood dripping from the body of the crucified Christ.

ERCOLE DE' ROBERTI
Ferrara 1451/1456–1496
Extinguishing a Fire (ca. 1473–1475).
Detail of the predella with *Miracles of St. Vincent Ferrer*. Panel: 10 1/2″ × 6′ 10 1/2″. Originally the predella belonged to the *Griffoni Polyptych*, formerly in S. Petronio, Bologna, then dismembered in the 18th century. Its principal panels are in Milan (Brera) and London (National Gallery); others are scattered among many public and private collections. The polyptych was commissioned from Francesco del Cossa, who executed personally the greater part of the panels. To his assistant, Ercole de' Roberti, he entrusted the predella and some of the small figures in the lateral pilasters.

ERCOLE DE' ROBERTI. *Miracles of St. Vincent Ferrer.*

Ercole de' Roberti, apprentice and protégé of Francesco del Cossa, collaborated with his master on the grandiose decoration in fresco of the *Salone dei Mesi* in Palazzo di Schifanoia, Ferrara, and later — between 1470 and 1475 — on the working out of the complex — dismembered in the 18th century — that was the *Griffoni Polyptych*. This work, whose dimensions and internal divisions were related to the Gothic structure of the chapels in S. Petronio, in the center had the image of St. Vincent Ferrer, and above a Crucifixion; while at the sides were figures of other saints, and in the predella scenes from the life of the saintly Dominican protagonist. The conception and design of the polyptych obviously belong to Francesco del Cossa, along with the painting of the larger panels, but in the small figures

ERCOLE DE' ROBERTI
Three Figures
Detail from predella with
Miracles of St. Vincent Ferrer.

of the pilasters and in the predella it is generally recognized that Ercole de' Roberti had the prominent hand. The assistant builds his narrative on a horizontal plane that is articulated by a succession of little temples, ruins, rows of columns, stairs and pavilions from one end to the other of the long panel, in keeping with the classical spirit of the architecture conjured up by Cossa in the upper panels. But his unrestrained invention is expressed in the broken and violent narration itself, in the inexhaustible repertory of details. The exorcisms, the healings and the other miracles worked by the saint proceed with unexpected starts and stops. Pebbles, chips, ends of beams, fragments of capitals and entablatures and cut stones litter the ground, protrude from walls or stratified rocks, hampering the action of the figures. Dressed in clothes that are wrinkled or curled up like metal strips, sometimes enlivened by details of unusual style recalling the extravagances of Gothic themes, they appear in conflicting attitudes: petrified in motionless positions — surly or distracted — or flung into a frantic race, straining forward in violent dashes.

FRA ANGELICO. *Frescoes in the Chapel of Nicholas V. The Lives of St. Stephen and St. Lawrence.* *pp. 142/145*

Fra Giovanni da Fiesole, called the Blessed Angelico or Fra Angelico, was summoned to Rome by Pope Eugene IV, and after the latter's death (1447) was kept in the service of his successor, Nicholas V. Fra Angelico was recalled to Florence in 1449 and made prior of the monastery of S. Marco, but in 1452 he returned to Rome, where he remained until his death (1455). Of the two cycles in the Vatican executed by the artist with the aid of Benozzo Gozzoli and five other assistants, that of the chapel of the Holy Sacrament is lost; the remaining cycle, representing *Scenes from the Lives of St. Stephen and St. Lawrence,* decorates the Chapel of Nicholas V, which the Pope intended for his own use as a place for privacy and study. Nicholas V (Tommaso Parentucelli), a man of broad cultural interests, promoter of numerous initiatives — not all of them came to anything — in the arts and letters and humanistic research, offered Fra Angelico, who was at the end of his career, the opportunity to give a further proof of his ability to sum up and utilize the results achieved in the art of painting in the present and the past.

After the lively colored "inlays" of the panels of his youth and early maturity, and after the bare depictions in the cells of S. Marco, the artist conjures up the scenes of the first Christian martyrs in a style of sustained dignity, placing the events in settings rich in historical evidence. A row of columns, pilasters decorated with scrolls and candelabra, the polished surfaces of a tower or a palace hark back to the grandeur of the Latin civilization with which Pope Nicholas hoped to re-establish a connection after overcoming the Schism of the West. To describe the events in the lives of the two saints with suitable nobility, the artist certainly returned to meditate on Masaccio's frescoes in the church of the Carmine, perhaps also taking into account the recent interpretation of Domenico Veneziano. Renouncing the splendor of the gold ground and the juxtaposition of pure colors, Fra Angelico here favors a clear, luminous elaboration of the color, in which white dominates in broad passages or emerges in the reds, greens and violets with changing effects.

FRA ANGELICO
(FRA GIOVANNI DA FIESOLE)
Fiesole 1387 — Rome 1455
Scenes from the Lives of St. Stephen and St. Lawrence: Detail of *St. Stephen Preaching* (ca. 1445–1455) Fresco: 8' 10" × 6' 7". The Chapel of Nicholas V was built as a place for his own meditation and study by Pope Nicholas V, who also commissioned its fresco decoration. Fra Angelico painted the walls of the chapel with the aid of Benozzo Gozzoli and five other assistants.

143

The compositional aim, closely tied to his intentions in regard to color, entirely absorbed the artist. Note in the *Preaching of St. Stephen* the motionless group of the onlookers, especially the women — of Giottesque solidity — closed without frills in their full mantles; or the silent ceremony of *Pope Sixtus II Gives St. Lawrence the Treasures of the Church for Distribution among the Poor,* treasures represented by a few objects reduced to polished abstract volumes: the swollen purse, the casket, two trays, four bowls and a silver ampulla, held by a young deacon. Finally there is the highly controlled portrayal of the crippled in *St. Lawrence Distributes the Treasures to the Poor;* the deformities and mutilations are barely indicated, and if a sly digression is met in the two smiling children, this is probably an addition by Gozzoli, who was very active in the execution of these frescoes, though within the conception and design of the master.

PINTURICCHIO. *Disputation of St. Catherine of Alexandria. The Borgia Apartments.* pp. 146/147
The fresco decoration of the Borgia Apartments was entrusted to Pinturicchio by Pope Alexander VI, and the name of the pontiff is usually cited to justify the representation of the *Disputation of St. Catherine* in the large lunette of the Sala dei Santi — the Hall of the Saints. There are those, however, who insinuate that in the choice of this saint, patron of bastards, is

FRA ANGELICO
*Scenes from the Lives of
St. Stephen and St. Lawrence.
St. Lawrence Distributes
Treasures to the Poor.*

144

FRA ANGELICO
*Scenes from the Lives of St. Stephen
and St. Lawrence.*
Detail: *Pope Sixtus II
Gives St. Lawrence Treasures for
Distribution among the Poor.*

concealed a veiled request for the protection of the Pope's numerous progeny. In any case, Pinturicchio, an enthusiastic portrayer of scenes and a master of great decorative effects, had no difficulty in unfolding before a broad landscape (dominated by the Borgia emblem, the bull atop a fantastic arch of triumph) the picturesque group of Oriental philosophers with the Emperor Maximinus presiding and the fragile Catherine before him. The saint counts the main points of her argument on her fingers, while a mixed crowd — contained on the right by the man in armor on a white horse — listens to the debate. Making full use of stucco relief and distributing a thick gold paste not only on the embroideries and the crowns but even on the architecture, the artist accentuates the theatrical taste of the composition, which is like a big "living picture" that has just been staged and will shortly be dispersed — demountable sets, rocks, ruins and backdrops all in wood and painted paper, costumes in silks and brocade to be put away and used on the next occasion.

The attempt to identify the figures in the fresco with historical personages has not given convincing results. To mention the non-demonstrable hypotheses, it has been proposed to recognize Lucrezia Borgia in St. Catherine; her brother Cesare in the Emperor; and Djem, the son of Mohammed II, an honored guest and hostage of the papal court, in the Turk with the big white turban. An identification that can, however, be made, is that of Pinturicchio and Antonio da Sangallo, on the extreme left.

PINTURICCHIO
(BERNARDINO DI BETTO)
Perugia 1454 — Siena 1513
Disputation of St. Catherine of Alexandria (1492–1494)
Fresco: 13' 10" × 26'.
Commissioned by Alexander VI; in the Hall of the Saints, Borgia Apartments.

PINTURICCHIO
Disputation of St. Catherine of Alexandria
Detail: *A Philosopher.*

TEMPLA DOMVM EXPOSITIS; VICOS FORA MOENIA PONTES:
VIRGINEAM TRIVII QVOD REPARARIS AQVAM.
PRISCA LICET NAVTIS STATVAS DARE COMMODA PORTVS:
ET VATICANVM CINGERE SIXTE IVGVM:
PLVS TAMEN VRBS DEBET: NAM QVAE SQVALORE LATEBAT:
CERNITVR IN CELEBRI BIBLIOTHECA LOCO.

MELOZZO DA FORLÍ. *Inauguration of the Vatican Library.*

The fresco, executed by Melozzo in his full maturity, clearly illustrates the artist's personal interpretation of the problems of perspective and the rigorous formulations of Piero della Francesca that he studied during his stay at Urbino. If Piero's expression is almost exclusively architectonic and spatial, linking human figures and architectural structures in a single discourse, Melozzo had other aims, and in this case composed a great marble framework obeying the optical perspective rules of Piero, but faced with variegated, colored areas and gilding to create a sumptuous setting worthy of a ceremony that took place in reality in July 1475. The scene in fact commemorates the occasion when Sixtus IV conferred the office of directing the Vatican Library on the humanist Bartolomeo Platina. The latter, shown kneeling, points to an inscription he composed which celebrates the urban improvements made by the Pope in the city of Rome. Also in attendance at the ceremony are the nephews of Sixtus IV: the Apostolic Protonotary, Rafaelle Riario (in profile); Giovanni della Rovere, Prefect of Rome, on the far left; next to him, Girolamo Riario, who was to become Governor of the

Pontifical States; in the center, imposing in cardinal's crimson, stands the future Julius II, whose bulk closes the view toward the vanishing point indicated by the profiles of the capitals and frames in the coffered ceiling. The interest in historical documentation, along with the taste for portraiture, probably came to Melozzo through acquaintanceship with another great interpreter of Piero della Francesca, Andrea Mantegna.

MELOZZO DA FORLÍ. *Angel Musician.*   *p. 149*

Little more remains of the fresco decoration executed by Melozzo in the apse of the church of the Holy Apostles than the 10 fragments (*Angels, Apostles,* the *Redeemer*) detached in 1711 when the tribune was demolished to enlarge the building. Vasari's description helps to reconstruct the composition of the fresco, which had a lower zone of painted architecture, the apostles in the foreground, Christ in the center with a thick band of cherubim, and around them the angel musicians. The total effect, however, which had been studied in relation to the curved surface of the support and the viewpoint of the spectator below, has been irremediably lost. Isolated fragments, like the angel illustrated here, with its profile clean cut against a cloud of blond hair, confirms Melozzo's predilection for compact forms and vibrant foreshortening, but do not allow us to reconstruct the bold conception and the exalted tone of the whole.

GIOVANNI BELLINI. *Pietà.*

The big altarpiece of the *Coronation of the Virgin*, executed around 1475 for the church of S. Giovanni Battista in Pesaro (now in the municipal museum) was surmounted by the *Pietà*, now in the Vatican Pinacoteca, which was obviously meant to be placed well above the spectator, as shown by the marked foreshortening. As in most of the works of his youth and early maturity, Bellini concentrates his expressive means on compositional values, avoiding any suggestion of dispersion, keeping the arms close to the bodies, entwining the hands and blocking off the drapery. The major inanimate element, the sober support for the group and starting point for the reading of the picture, is the fluted edge of the sarcophagus on which Christ is seated. From here the movement of the group is articulated in terms of broad angles, as in the bent arms of Christ and Nicodemus, who is holding Him. It extends upward with the obliquely placed torso of Joseph of Arimethea. Joseph's bowed head, framed by the large black beard, stops the movement and it not descends, touching the unguent pot and following the direction of the Magdalen's glance towards the knot of hands — the bruised hands of Christ, the worn hands of the woman. The suspended cradle of fingers sums up the sense of the perfectly sealed composition, and the subtlety of the nuances of color calls our attention to the originality of the color scheme. The elegant harmony between yellow, white, violet and tawny, warm browns, changing under the drenching ray of light, confirms that the artist had gone beyond the early influence of Mantegna. The forms he had expressed in the preceding decades in structural terms he now develops with pictorial and coloristic means.

150

GIOVANNI BELLINI
Venice 1430 (?)–1516
Pietà (ca. 1470–1475)
Panel: 41 3/4" × 33". Provenance: Aldovrandi collection, Bologna. Originally surmounted the large altarpiece of the *Coronation of the Virgin*, now in the Pinacoteca of Pesaro.

LEONARDO. *St. Jerome.*

The panel, which was sawn in two at an unknown date, was put together by chance in the 19th century by Cardinal Fesch, who found the first half at a junkman's, where it was used as the lid of a box; and five years later the second, at a shoemaker's. The painting belongs to Leonardo's first Florentine period, and is contemporary with or a little later than the the large *Adoration of the Magi* in the Uffizi. The figures of the saint about to beat his breast and of the lion curling his tail like a whip are diagonally placed in a rocky landscape. Without any form of introduction or accent to lead into the composition, the images almost spring up from the bleak earth and twist forward towards the light. The movement is intensified in the sorrowful head — the eye sockets, the black gash of the mouth — of the hollow-cheeked saint. The rejection of any traditional composition is reflected in the pictorial technique, for the monochrome impasto in the ocher tones does not fill the contours but is built up on an outline sketch, defining the spatial relationships by graduated passages from dark to light. Note how the lion measures the extent of the space in the foreground with the reversed curves of the tail and the hindquarters, and the density of the empty space embraced by the knee and bent arm of the saint. In the background, to the right, is the sketch of a cathedral; to the left, veiled blue-green transparencies evoke distant shores.

152

LEONARDO DA VINCI
Vinci 1452 — Amboise 1519
St. Jerome (ca. 1482)
Panel: 40 1/2″ × 30″.
Provenance: collection of Cardinal Fesch, Napoleon's uncle.

RAPHAEL
Madonna of Foligno (1511–1512)
Panel transferred to canvas: 10′ 6″ × 6′ 4″.
Commissioned by Sigismondo Conti for the
church of S. Maria di Aracoeli, it was then
donated to the Convent of S. Anna in Foligno in 1565, at the request of a grand-
daughter of Conti, the abbess of the convent. Confiscated by the French in 1797, it
was restored to them and subsequently — in
1815 — returned to Italy.

RAPHAEL
Madonna of Foligno
Detail: *St. John the Baptist and St. Francis.*

RAPHAEL. *Madonna of Foligno.*

The panel was dedicated to the Virgin by the humanist Sigismondo Conti,
secretary to Pope Julius II, as a mark of gratitude for the protection accorded his house in Foligno, which had been struck by lightning but was
undamaged. Conti is portrayed kneeling as he is presented by St. Jerome;
to the left are St. Francis and St. John the Baptist; in the center Sigismondo's house, emerging from the mists and the greenish hills, is surmounted
by the parabolic curve of the rainbow, and the orange globe of the thunder-
bolt is about to hit it. Above, in a nimbus surrounded by a host of blue
cherubim, are the Madonna and the Child. The arched form of the panel
and the corresponding curves of the golden nimbus, the rainbow and the
grassy areas in the foreground show that the artist wished to enclose figures
and environment in a compact organization, transferring the crystalline con-
structions of the kind he studied in Piero dela Francesca and Perugino to a
monumental dimension. It is during these years, when the great enterprise
of the Vatican Stanze (1510–1511) was well advanced, that Raphael lived
the most intense period of his brief, meteoric career. Brimming with Umbrian and Tuscan culture, he had moved to Rome, perhaps having sensed the
symptoms of retrenchment and crisis in the Florentine world. In Rome he

155

became aware of the different stylistic currents popularized by such artists as Sodoma, Bramantino, Sebastiano del Piombo, Lorenzo Lotto, Dosso and Battista Dossi. Decisive new impulses were given to the works of many of these painters by Raphael's solutions. He in turn was not indifferent to what he saw in their work, and in this painting the influence of the new Venetian color — of Bellini and Giorgione — is apparent. It is seen in the moist landscape, in the surfaces full of tonal passages which soften the supporting composition — surfaces that are more compact than ever and shining in warm browns of the flesh, in greys and silvery blues, in sumptuous reds.

RAPHAEL. *Transfiguration.*

Cardinal Giulio de' Medici, having obtained the archbishopric of Narbonne from Francis I, commissioned Sebastiano del Piombo to paint a *Resurrection of Lazarus* and Raphael this *Transfiguration,* intending both pictures for the cathedral of that city. As is well known, Raphael gave absolute and exclusive value to the conception, plan and composition of a work, in the certainty that the participation of collaborators in the material execution did not invalidate the presence of the master's genius. That this was his conviction is corroborated by the gift he made to Dürer of a drawing with his sig-

RAPHAEL
Urbino 1482 — Rome 1520
Transfiguration (1519–1520)
Panel: 13' 3" × 9' 2".
After the premature death of Raphael, Cardinal Giulio de' Medici, who commissioned this work, decided not to send it to Narbonne, as he had done with the *Resurrection of Lazarus,* which had been executed at the same time by Sebastiano del Piombo, for the cathedral of that city. He kept it for several years in his Palazzo della Cancelleria, then gave it to the church of S. Pietro in Montorio, Rome. The French confiscated it in 1797 and took it to Paris, where it was restored; it was returned to the Vatican in 1815.

RAPHAEL
Transfiguration
Detail: *Christ with the Prophets Elijah and Moses.*

CARAVAGGIO
(MICHELANGELO MERISI)
Caravaggio 1573 — Porto Ercole 1610
Deposition of Christ (1602–1604) Canvas:
9' 10" × 6' 8". Commissioned by Pietro
Vittrice for his family chapel in S. Maria
in Valicella, Rome, where it was already
installed in 1604.

nature, which in reality was executed by Giulio Romano. However, because of criticisms at the papal court concerning this practice — perhaps because of the intervention of artists with different training, accustomed to other techniques, like Sebastiano del Piombo — while a large band of assistants was completing the decoration of the Stanze, Raphael decided to execute the *Transfiguration* personally. He began it in 1519; in April of the following year he was seized with a violent fever and in a few days died, leaving the lower part of the painting unfinished. Following the lines of his sketch, Giulio Romano and Francesco Penni completed the picture.

The work has aroused conflicting opinions. Some critics have emphasized the importance of the interruption caused by the death of the master, ascribing decisive weight — in the negative sense — to the assistants' contribution. Today, after mature critical appraisal, the validity of the dense compositional and symbolist program and the expressive intensity of the final result, no matter how achieved, are recognized. The central nucleus of the Raphaelesque idea is represented here by a radial module having its center in the "platform" occupied by the three dazzled apostles (Peter, James and John). Above them the limitless expansion of the same radial motive is seen in the flashing explosion of Christ poised in mid-air, flanked by Elijah and Moses. At the foot of Mount Tabor the scene of the boy possessed, surrounded by members of his family and other apostles, takes its place in the dramatic intensity of the event, the figures mobilized in a series of impetuous movements that connect with the triad suspended in the sphere of light.

CARAVAGGIO. *Deposition of Christ.*

Among the works that may be securely attributed to Caravaggio, this *Deposition* is the only example of a subject that must have been congenial to the formal inclinations of the artist, both in the relations of strength between the figures receiving and laying down a lifeless body, and in the possibilities for contrast in material and color between the traditionally clothed figures — Nicodemus, St. John the Evangelist, the Virgin, the Marys — and the nude, shrouded Christ. It is known how much importance in organizing the image Caravaggio gave to the use of whites. The *Deposition* is one of the most fully achieved works of the painter's maturity. And if it aroused some dissent among contemporary scholars — because of an alleged lack of decorum, an argument that was revived in the 19th century — it has otherwise been appreciated and studied as one of the fundamental "texts" in painting, by the artists of every period, including Rubens and Cézanne, who copied it or reflected its influence.

The base of the group articulated in leaps and stops, is the slab that aggressively points a corner towards us. On it fall the hand of Jesus and an edge of the winding sheet, which visually leads back to the livid torso and the heads of St. John and Nicodemus, who are holding Christ tightly as in a vice. This is the point of maximum tension in the picture, which takes on live sculptural form in the heavy-set figure of the old man, while contrasts between the dark green, the red, the bright brown on the one hand, and the ivory and white on the other, become violent. The shadow thickens on the faces of the bowed heads of the Virgin and the Magdalen, but at the apex of the composition the broad gesture of Mary Salome liberates the upward movements.

On page 160:
CARAVAGGIO
Deposition of Christ
Detail: *Jesus and
St. John the Baptist.*

159

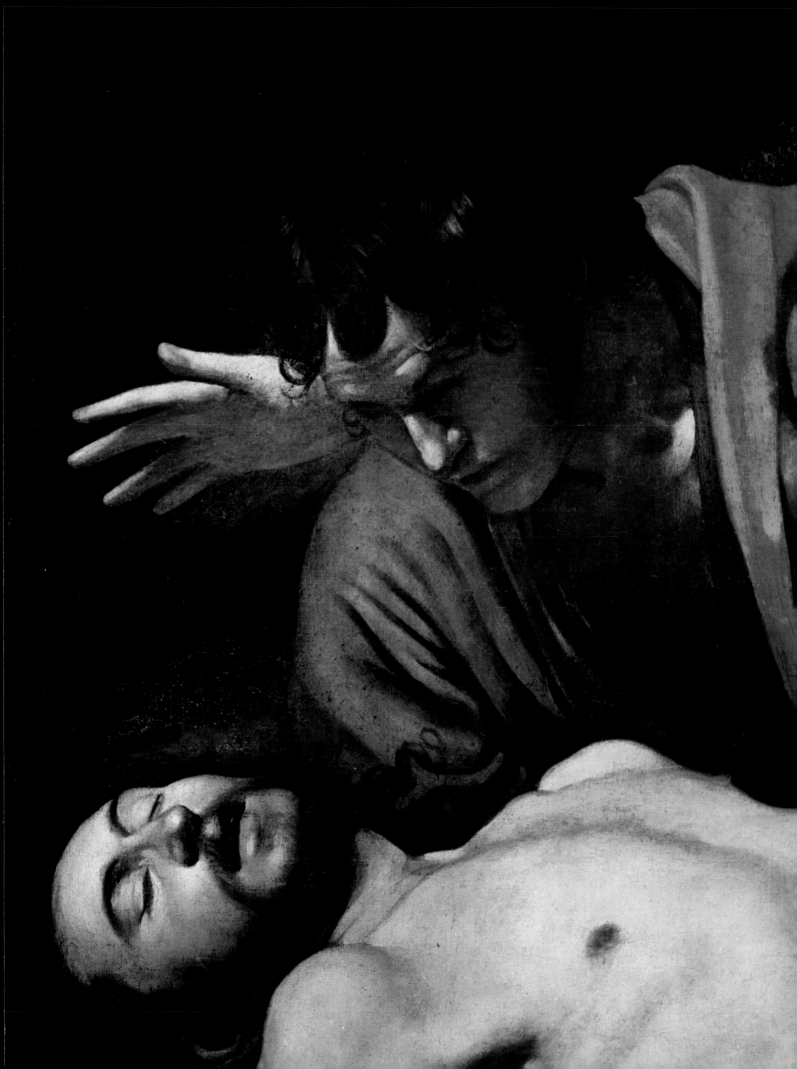

HISTORY OF THE MUSEUMS
AND THEIR BUILDINGS

HISTORY OF THE COLLECTIONS

The ensemble of the Vatican collections is a unique testimony to the splendor and power of one of the most important European courts of all times. Indeed it continued to enrich itself with magnificence equal to and greater than that of the "temporal" courts even when it had lost most of its tangible political power.

The Vatican collections differ from the other great princely collections, which later became the cores of museums like the Louvre and the Uffizi, by the fact that they were put together at the desire of successive popes who came from Italian families that were already themselves outstanding in regard to the history and habit of collecting. The papacy has had the exceptional advantage of ready access, by right of ownership, not only to the treasures of Early Christian art, that is objects found in the numerous Roman catacombs and works of art in the churches under Vatican hegemony (St. Peter's itself and St. John Lateran), but also to a large part of the choice archeological discoveries in Rome during the centuries when the city was under the jurisdiction of the Church. The collections are thus made up of objects and works of the first importance in the history of ancient and modern art.

This great heritage is composed of the collections of painting, sculpture and other objects, of the very rich Vatican Library, and of the various halls and places (not including the Basilica of St. Peter) which the popes had decorated at different times, for example the Borgia Apartments and the Sistine Chapel. The collections have had a rather adventurous history, since on no less than three occasions they suffered more or less serious damage because of wars and political vicissitudes. The first loss, sustained during the Babylonian Captivity — the removal to Avignon — in the 14th century, meant that after almost a century of absence from Rome the popes had in fact to start the collections again from the beginning. Then came the Sack of Rome in 1527 by the troops of Charles V; and in the 19th century there was the occupation by Napoleon's troops. The present collections go back to the end of the Schism of the West (1418) and represents the efforts of the great popes of the 15th and 16th centuries. The greater part of the collections, however, was created in the 18th century, under the stimulus of the Enlightenment and the new interest in archeology and museums. At the end of that century the Vatican Museums consisted of the Museo Pio-Clementino for sculpture, the Library with the annexed Museo Sacro, Museo Profano, Gallery of Inscriptions, the Medal and Coin Cabinet and the Pontifical Apartments. The Pinacoteca or picture gallery, created — along with other collections — in the 19th century, was given its present form in the course of this century. As we are dealing not with a single museum divided into departments, but with entirely separate museums, which have developed independently, the history of their formation will be treated in connection with a description of their contents.

The Vatican Library

The Vatican Library was the first nucleus of the pontifical collections, having been founded by Nicholas V (1447–1455) with the heritage of the old libraries of the popes. The 15th century was a period of great bibliophilia, and popes like Nicholas V himself (who on his death had increased the collection by 1,200 volumes), Pius II (1458–1464) and Sixtus IV (1471–1484) surrounded themselves with the most celebrated scholars and humanists. Sixtus IV doubled the collection and charged Bartolomeo Platina with its arrangement. In the course of the 16th century the Library was enriched with many printed books, and under Sixtus V (1585–1590) was definitively installed in new quarters. In the 17th century it was enlarged by several very important private gifts and bequests of manuscripts, such as the Fondo Palatino, donated by Maximilian I of Bavaria to Gregory XV in 1623 (2,037 codices), the Fondo Urbinate, acquired by Alexander VII (1,799 codices) and the Fondo Reginense, acquired by Alexander VIII, most of whose 2,120 codices came from the library of Queen Christina of Sweden. A plan was made in the 18th century for the publication of a complete catalogue of what had become a vast collection, but of the 20 volumes projected only four saw print (1756–1768). Meanwhile other collections were acquired, and in the 19th century catalogues and scientific descriptions of the various groups of manuscripts were compiled.

The present Library contains 12 collections of manuscripts (about 50,000) acquired for the most part from papal families, such as the Capponi, Barberini, Ottoboni, Chigi and so on. In addition there are 13 groups in the stacks that come from the archives of various churches, about 800,000 printed books, 100,000 prints and 7,000 incunabula. There are various special sections, such as that of the papyri (the first were acquired by Paul V at the beginning of the 17th century), that of the music manuscripts (dating as early as the 9th century and coming from Lorsch, Evreux etc., and from the Sistine and Julian Chapels), palimpsests, autographs (Michelangelo, Luther, Tasso, Thomas Aquinas, etc.) drawings (among which a part of the *Divine Comedy* illustrated by Botticelli) and caricatures (the famous notebooks of Bernini and of Pier Leone Ghezzi).

The Museo Sacro

A library, according to the old conception, included not only books but also curios and objects of artistic and scientific interest. The Vatican Library is the ideal example of this kind of collection, created in the climate of the Enlightenment, when the enthusiasm for archeology, already apparent in the taste of the scholars of the 16th and 17th centuries, combined with the new consciousness of history which developed in the 18th century. In fact the Library had no less than three annexed museums: the Museo Sacro, the Museo Profano and the Medal and Coin Cabinet, the results of the felicitous acquisitions made by Clement XI (1730–1740) and Benedict XIV (1740–1758). After acquiring several splendid collections, such as the Carpegna (notable for Early Christian objects found in the catacombs), the Vettori (mainly ancient gems), the Buonaccolti (Early Christian glass) and the famous medal and coin collection of Cardinal Albani, Benedict XIV commissioned Scipione Maffei to design the Museo Sacro, which was constructed in 1755–56. To this initial group of objects were gradually added other important collections (those of Francesco Gori, Giuseppe Bianchi and of Pope Benedict himself). The whole ensemble was reorganized in 1937, and today the museum consists primarily of ivories (156 pieces, including the *Lorsch Diptych*), bronzes and thousands of terra cottas, constituting the largest such collection in the world.

The Museo Profano

The Museo Profano arose out of the collections mentioned above, having been instituted by the Cardinal Librarian Domenico Passionei in 1761 to house the objects not belonging to the practice of Christianity or the Early Christian period. Although the museum lost a large part of its contents (the whole of the Albani medal and coin collection) in 1798, during the French invasion, it was refurnished from the excavations that were carried out in Rome between 1809 and 1815. It too was reorganized in 1937, and today includes gems, glass, mosaics, etc., of Roman and Etruscan times. Renaissance objects have been removed from the museum for exhibition in the Borgia Apartments.

The Medal and Coin Cabinet

The *Medagliere,* or medal and coin collection, one of the richest in the world, was probably based on the 16th-century cabinet of Cardinal Marcello Cervino, and in any case included the splendid Albani collection (1738). It was enlarged by the addition of the Carpegna, Scilla and Odescalchi collections (the last included a large part of Queen Christina's *medagliere*). Scattered during the Napoleonic occupation, the *Medagliere* was established again in the 19th century with the Vitali collection (1807) and other important private bequests and gifts, as well as a considerable part of the Propaganda Fide medal and coin cabinet. Today it contains more than 100,000 pieces, divided into two main groups: Roman coins and papal coinage.

The Museo Pio-Clementino

The Museo Pio-Clementino, which goes back to the collection started by Julius II (1503–1513) at the beginning of the 16th century (kept in the Cortile del Belvedere and on the Capitoline until the 18th century), is the pontifical collection of ancient sculpture. The museum was founded during the pontificate of Clement XIV (1769–1774), was enlarged by Pius VI (1775–1779) and had its definitive organization at that time. It includes a number of masterpieces of Greek and Roman sculpture, such as the *Apollo Belvedere,* the *Laocoön,* the *Belvedere Torso,* the *Venus of Cnidus* and a vast number of other statues, busts and mosaics.

The Museo Chiaramonti

The Museo Chiaramonti was established by Pope Pius VII (1800–1824) and owes its Neo-Classic decor to the sculptor Antonio Canova. It, too, is devoted to ancient art, and consists of three parts: the Museum, in the corridor designed by Bramante; the Braccio Nuovo — New Wing — housing some of the major pieces (like the *Augustus of Prima Porta*); and the Gallery of Inscriptions (*Galleria Lapidaria*) which is unrivaled for the number of ancient inscriptions.

The Etruscan Museum

The Museo Gregoriano Etrusco was created by Gregory XVI (1831–1846) in 1836, in response to the ever increasing interest in archeology which began in the 18th century with the Museo Pio-Clementino, continued in the 19th with the Museo Chiaramonti and then had ramified to include the new field of Etruscology, the phase of antiquity most in vogue at the time. In fact the museum was established with the material obtained from the excavations made in southern Etruria from 1828 onwards, to which were added other objects that had been part of the Library's collections. Here among numerous other things are shown the contents of the Regolini-Galassi Tomb, discovered intact in 1936 at Cerveteri, and the famous *Warrior from Todi,* found in the Umbrian city in 1835. Many of the other objects come from Vulci and from excavations at Bomarzo and Orte. The museum was reorganized in 1924.

The Egyptian Museum

The Egyptian Museum was instituted by Gregory XVI and opened to the public in 1839. It includes all of the Egyptian objects from the collections earlier exhibited in the Vatican and on the Capitoline, as well as the material found at Hadrian's Villa. Organized by Luigi M. Ungarelli, one of the first Italian followers of the noted French Egyptologist, Champollion, it was enlarged with private collections and objects brought back to Italy by missionaries.

The Vatican Pinacoteca

The Pinacoteca is one of the most recent museums in the Vatican complex, and was inaugurated in its present quarters in 1932. It was created in the midst of dramatic events following the Treaty of Tolentino in 1797, by which 100 paintings and 64 sculptures were removed from the Vatican by Napoleon (among them, Raphael's *Transfiguration* and Caravaggio's *Deposition of Christ*). After the French defeat, Pius II sent Antonio Canova (who had been Inspector General of Fine Arts since 1802) to Paris to ask for the return of these works. The famous sculptor's mission had some success, considering that in October 1816 more than half of the paintings and sculptures were returned to Rome.

This first group, together with other works from the old pontifical collections that had been in storage, was first arranged in the Borgia Apartments, and the first guide to the collection came out in 1821. However by 1822 the picture collection had already been moved to the apartments of Gregory XIII and then in 1836 to those of Pius V. After a further change (again to Gregory XIII's apartments, though these are small and are difficult for the public to reach), Pius X decided in 1909 to create a new picture gallery and chose for it some premises to the west of the Cortile del Belvedere. Only 20 years later it was decided to give the Pinacoteca its present independent quarters.

While these moves were taking place, the Pinacoteca continued to grow, especially in the second half of the 19th century. Leo XII had already enriched the collection with the *Sixtus IV* fresco by Melozzo da Forlí, and Leo XIII with the Gentile da Fabriano *Triptych*. Pius IX acquired seven works, among them the *St. Jerome* by Leonardo, and made gifts of a Crivelli and a Guercino. Pius X added various works, removed from the private apartments of the Vatican, from the Lateran, the Library and the Museo Cristiano, bringing the number of pictures up to 277. With the new quarters it was possible to double this figure, by including paintings from papal residences including Castelgandolfo. Thus the Pinacoteca acquired works by Bernardo Daddi, Giovanni di Paolo, Scarsellino, Girolamo Muziano, Pier Francesco Mola and Francesco Solimena. With the addition of the Russian and Byzantine paintings the Pinacoteca assumed, under the Pontificate of Pius XII, its present form. In 1956 a separate section was set up for contemporary art.

Services

The Vatican Museums have their own laboratory for restoring paintings, sculptures and objects, and a photographic department. Temporary exhibitions of objects and documents are occasionally put on.

THE BUILDINGS

The history of the buildings that house the Vatican Museums, and include the decorated apartments and chapels, is extremely complicated, since there has been no period from the 15th century to our day when there has been no building activity going on. The vast ensemble came into being with the reconstruction of St. Peter's in the 15th century. Before this time the residential accommodations at the Vatican must have been insignificant, and until the Babylonian Captivity at Avignon the popes preferred the Lateran as the center of their activities.

The first reorganization of the Apostolic palaces and galleries was undertaken by Nicholas V, who added to what remained of the 13th-century buildings the part of the palace giving on the Cortile di San Damaso, and made a chapel (which he had Fra Angelico fresco) in a tower constructed at the time of Nicholas III. In this way a four-sided complex was formed, to which Sixtus IV added the Sistine Chapel, built in the next to the last decade of the 15th century by Giovannino de' Dolci and decorated by the best-known painters of the day.

Innocent VIII had the Palazzetto del Belvedere built on plans by Antonio del Pollaiuolo. Here is the beginning of the impressive prospect later developed by Bramante during the pontificate of Julius II (1503–1513) when he joined the Palazzetto to the main palaces by means of a long corridor in which the Museo Chiaramonti was subsequently arranged.

Meanwhile Alexander VI (1492–1503) had had his apartments decorated, and Julius II, with the refined taste of one of the greatest art patrons of the Renaissance, had his Stanze frescoed by Raphael. In the time of Julius II and Leo X, some of the most celebrated artists of the century worked in the Vatican palaces — Bramante, Raphael and Michelangelo. To the first two we owe the Logge and the Stanze, to the last the decoration of the Sistine Chapel ceiling and later the *Last Judgment* on the rear wall of the chapel; as well as the frescoes of the Pauline Chapel, ordered by Pope Paul III (1534–1550).

Gregory XIII (1572–1585) was responsible for many of the stucco and painted decorations of the palace dating from the second half of the 16th century, and above all the beautiful Gallery of the Maps (Galleria delle Carte Geographiche). His successor, Sixtus IV (1585–1590), had the architect Domenico Fontana build the new premises for the Library. This required the construction of a wing cutting across the Cortile del Belvedere where there was a change in ground level, and thus created two smaller courtyards. To Fontana we also owe the part of the Apostolic Palace which we see from St. Peter's Square.

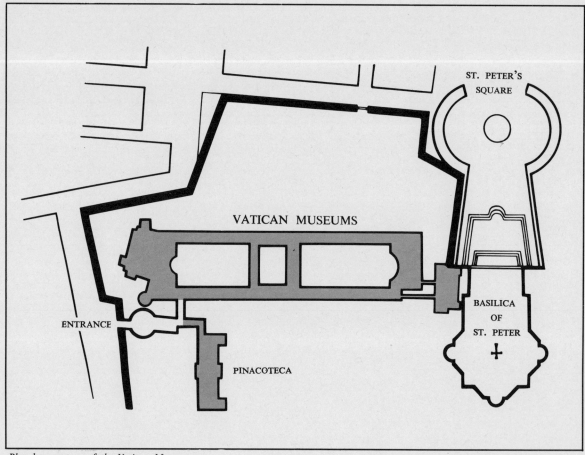

Plan by courtesy of the Vatican Museum.

While the 17th century is to be remembered for progress on the building of St. Peter's, in the 18th century interest revived in the Vatican palaces, no longer considered as residences or places to receive people, but as proper museums. The complex of galleries built on to the Palazzetto, at the behest of Clement XIV and Pius VI, contains the sculpture museum that bears their names. The architects were Michele Simonetti and Giuseppe Camporesi, who produced a notable example of Neo-Classical style conforming to the best 18th-century museum standards. From 1817 to 1822 Rafaello Stern built the New Wing of the Museo Chiaramonti, which lay parallel to Fontana's Library and divided the Cortile del Belvedere into three parts. In the fourth decade of the 19th century the halls of the future Egyptian Museum were redecorated in a Neo-Egyptian style.

In this century the problem of creating a single entrance providing access to all the museums and the decorated apartments, was resolved by the construction of the double spiral staircase leading to the Museo Pio-Clementino and the Egyptian Museum on one side, and to the Pinacoteca on the other. This arrangement was conceived at the time of the construction of the new Vatican Pinacoteca, which was inaugurated in 1932.

FIRST FLOOR

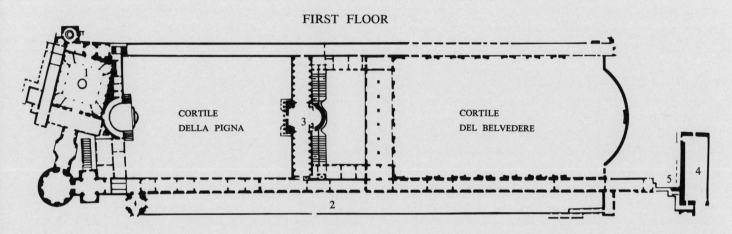

LEGEND

CORTILE OTTAGONO	1
LIBRARY	2
BRACCIO NUOVO (NEW WING)	3
SISTINE CHAPEL	4
STAIRS TO SISTINE	5
CHAPEL OF NICHOLAS V	6
SALONE DI COSTANTINO	7
RAPHAEL'S LOGGIA	8
STANZA DELLA SEGNATURA	9
STANZA DI ELIODORO	10
STANZA DELL'INCENDIO DI BORGO	11

SECOND FLOOR

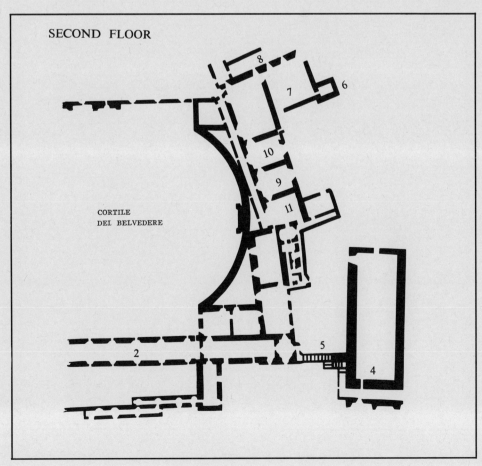

SELECTED BIBLIOGRAPHY

GENERAL READING

CORRADO RICCI AND OTHERS: *The Vatican: its History, its Treasures.* (New York, 1914).

CARLO CECCHELLI: *Il Vaticano, la Basilica, i Palazzi, i Giardini, le mura.* (Rome, 1928).

G. BARDI: *Origine e sviluppo del Musei e Gallerie pontificie.* (Rome, 1948).

BARTOLOMMEO NOGARA: *Tesori d'arte del Vaticano.* (Bergamo, 1950).

LUDWIG VON PASTOR: *The History of the Popes from the Close of the Middle Ages.* (London 1896 ff.).

G. COLONNA, M. DONATI, D. REDIG DE CAMPOS: *Musei Vaticani.* (Novara, 1962).

D. REDIG DE CAMPOS: *Palazzi Vaticani.* (Bologna, 1967).

GUIDES AND DESCRIPTIONS OF THE MUSEUMS

FILIPPO AURELIO VISCONTI AND GIURSEPPE ANTONIO GUATTANI: *Il Museo Pio-Clementino.* (2 vols. Rome, 1782, 1807).

Il Museo Chiaramonti. (3 vols. Rome, 1808, 1817, 1843).

XAVIER BARBIER DE MONTAULT: *La Bibliothèque Vaticane et ses annexes.* (Rome, 1867).

ORAZIO MARUCCHI: *Il Museo Egizio Vaticano descritto e illustrato.* (Rome, 1902).

GIOVANNI PINZA: *Materiali per la etnologia antica toscane e laziale del Museo Gregoriano Etrusco.* (Milan, 1915).

BARTOLOMMEO NOGARA: *Guida del Museo Vaticano di Scultura.* (Rome, 1924).

Catologo delle Riproduzioni Fototipiche e Plastiche (with list of publications concerning the Vatican Library and connected museums) (Vatican City, 1943).

ENNIO FRANCIA: *Tesori della Pinacoteca Vaticana.* (Rome, 1965).

DEOCLÉCIO REDIG DE CAMPOS: *Wanderings among Vatican Paintings.* (Del Turco, Rome, 1961).

DEOCLÉCIO REDIG DE CAMPOS: *Sistine Chapel.* (Istituto Geografico, Novara, 1959).

MAURIZIO CALVESI: *Treasures of the Vatican.* (Skira, Geneva and New York, 1962).

KARL IPSER: *Vatican Art.* (Philosophical Library, New York, 1953).

For his courtesy in furnishing information of great value for the preparation of this book, we wish to thank Dr. Deoclécio Redig de Campos, Inspector of the Vatican Museums.

INDEX OF ILLUSTRATIONS

INDEX OF NAMES

GENERAL INDEX